MW01531907

I CAN DO THIS!

McDougal & Associates
Servants of Christ and stewards of the mysteries of God

I CAN DO THIS!

OVERCOMING LIFE'S SEEMINGLY IMPOSSIBLE SITUATIONS

HAROLD McDOUGAL

Unless otherwise noted, all Scripture references are from The New Living Translation of the Bible, copyright © 1996 by Tyndale House Publishers, Inc., Wheaton, Illinois. References marked KJV are from the King James Version of the Bible. References marked NKJ are from the New King James Version of the Bible © copyright 1979, 1980, 1982 by Thomas Nelson, Inc., Nashville, Tennessee. References marked AMPLIFIED are from the Amplified Bible, © copyright 1987 by the Zondervan Corporation and the Lockman Foundation, La Habra, California.

I CAN DO THIS!: OVERCOMING LIFE'S SEEMINGLY IMPOSSIBLE SITUATIONS
Copyright © 2008—Harold McDougal

No part of this book may be reproduced or transmitted in any form or by any means, electronic or mechanical, including photocopying, recording, or by any information retrieval system.

Cover design by Sherie Campbell
sonandshield@comcast.net

Published by:

McDougal & Associates
Greenwell Springs, LA 70739-0194
www.thepublishedword.com

McDougal & Associates is dedicated to the spreading of the Gospel of Jesus Christ to as many people as possible in the shortest time possible.

ISBN 13: 978-1-934769-02-7
ISBN 10: 1-934769-02-9

Printed in the United States of America
For Worldwide Distribution

DEDICATION

To all those who know what it is to struggle to make it through each and every new day.

For I can do everything with the help of Christ who gives me the strength I need.
Philippians 4:13

Anything is possible if a person believes.
Mark 9:23

CONTENTS

INTRODUCTION

"I can do this!"

When we say things like this, is it just what we commonly call "hype?" Are we just "psyching ourselves up" to do better than we really think we can? Is it just another false expectation that will fail like others before it and which, therefore, is just setting us up for even more heartache? If we speak such words and have nothing to back them up, that may well be the case. Boasting to ourselves or to others of what we can do often ends in little more than added disappointment.

There is an awful lot in life that we seemingly cannot do—feelings that we cannot seem to conquer, relationships that we cannot seem to get right, assigned tasks that we cannot seem to finish (or sometimes even get started), goals that seem elusive, dreams that seem to float away with the wind, desires that remain locked up in our inner self. There is so much that we *want* to do in life, but when we start trying to actually *do* it, it's not nearly as easy as we thought it would be, and we often fail.

We not only fail; we fail miserably. It's not just that we cannot fly; we can't even get off of the ground. It's not that we can't finish projects; we can't even seem to get them started. It's not just that we can't seem to resolve problems.; many times we can't even understand what the problem is. Life has a way of throwing us curve balls that, for various reasons, we seem incapable of hitting.

And so the hours pass, the days, the weeks, the months and the years, and suddenly we find ourselves facing the truth that life is somehow passing us by, and we don't know how to grab it by the coattails. We know what we want in our hearts, but we don't know how to get it. Often we even know what God wants for us, but that also proves to be elusive.

So what are we doing wrong? Are we unique in our frustration, or are these things that all men and women everywhere face? The Bible answers these questions in a very wonderful way. It actually takes us inside the personal lives of many men and women of different generations. It lets us see them in the midst of their battles. It lets us see them flailing around for answers to life's dilemmas. And it even lets us see them failing.

I love that about the Bible. It's so real. It doesn't hide any of the warts or the freckles. It's all there in plain view for us to see.

When we begin to read the pages of Genesis, for instance, we first see the powerful and moving description of creation. But, then, before long, there appear Cain and Abel, with their sibling jealousies and the resulting tragic murder of Abel and Cain's banishment. Now that's real!

Why does the Bible do that? Why does it describe to

us in such lurid detail the failings of men like Moses, David and even Peter? We need to look up to these men, for they actually wrote much of the Bible. And can we look up to them when they failed so miserably? This is an important issue and one that we all need to understand.

This is precisely the point. These were real people, people with daily struggles, people with challenges, people with enemies of every kind. And yet they each found a key that enabled them to cope with the impossible situations of their daily life.

Where to start in presenting a review of such Bible characters is not an easy question, but the book of Hebrews contains a whole chapter dedicated to stories just like these. There, in chapter 11, some Old Testament lives are encapsulated in just a few verses, some in only one verse, and others in just a few simple words. For most of the ancients, we can add to what is said in Hebrews 11 from the historical accounts of other portions of the Bible. There, many chapters are dedicated to some men and women of old.

So, now let us take a journey of faith. And as we thrill anew at the exploits of God's heroes of faith, let us feel our own faith growing so that we can overcome the impossible circumstances of *our* daily lives and as a result, let us go forth to do exploits of our own in this very exciting time in which we are living. God has promised that we can do such exploits, for He—the God of Abraham, Isaac, Jacob, Elisha, Gideon and David—is our God too, and He has declared that for those who believe, *"everything is possible."* Therefore, we can say without question, *"I Can Do This!"* And then we can go out and do it in Jesus' name. Let's begin the journey.

Harold McDougal
Alexandria, Virginia

PART I

WHAT WILL IT TAKE TO OVERCOME YOUR DAILY TRIALS

CHAPTER 1

CAN IT BE THAT SIMPLE?

What is faith? It is the confident assurance that what we hope for is going to happen. It is the evidence of things we cannot yet see.   Hebrews 11:1

What is the key to overcoming? Paul wrote, *"I can do everything"* (Philippians 4:13), but he didn't end it there. He said, *"I can do everything with the help of Christ."* It is evident from this that overcoming is not something we can do on our own. With God's help, we can overcome. If we insist on trying it without His help, we're on our own.

And how do we tap into God's strength? It can only be done by faith. Jesus said it all when He declared: *"Anything is possible if a person believes"* (Mark 9:23). Believes in what? Believes in himself? Believes in his future?

Believes in his own ability? Clearly the faith we need must be directed to the proper Source—God Himself.

No Bible Theme Could Be More Important

Faith ... No Bible theme could be more important. We are saved by faith, we receive healing by faith, we get answers to our prayers by faith, the gifts of the Spirit and the various ministries operate by faith, and God supplies our daily material needs when we demonstrate faith in Him. Without faith, we cannot even please Him, and the writer of the Hebrews confirmed it:

Faith is not a complicated concept in any sense of the word!

It is impossible to please God without faith.   Hebrews 11:6

The faith that we demonstrate toward God must be of the simple variety. This is made clear by the fact that throughout the centuries our Lord has often used very humble people. In the time of Jesus, for example, the Pharisees would seem to have been the logical choice to become apostles of the newly-formed Church. They were dedicated, disciplined and studious people. Instead, Jesus chose unlearned fishermen and a despised tax collector. Why? The Pharisees were so intellectually prepared that they could not accept the simple truths that Jesus put forth. His teachings were too easy for them, so they couldn't take Him seriously. Nothing can replace simple faith in God.

In this famous eleventh chapter of Hebrews, we cannot help but notice that many great generals are absent from the list, as are many politicians, poets and philosophers. Instead, in the list we find a former prostitute, a foreigner and a shepherd boy. In the end, every man or woman was judged by history according to whether or not he demonstrated faith in God.

God gave his approval to people in days of old because of their faith.   Hebrews 11:2

Wow! This is an important subject. And, since it will affect the outcome of your daily struggle with life's challenges, that makes it all the more important.

FAITH IS NOT A COMPLICATED CONCEPT

Faith is not a complicated concept in any sense of the word. It's so easy to understand, in fact, that a child can comprehend it. It is this simplicity that creates a problem for many. To them, faith seems too simple to be true, so they feel compelled to complicate it. Simply stated, faith means believing, and faith in God means believing God. Simple faith is an unrestrained and uncluttered faith, a childlike faith, that makes possible the fulfillment of the promise and potential God has for each of our lives. Jesus said:

To all who believed him and accepted him, he gave the right to become children of God.   John 1:12

The King James Version of the Bible says it this way:

But as many as received him, to them gave he power to become the sons of God, even to them that believe on [or have faith in] *his name:*

The Amplified Bible rendering of this same verse shows the variety of meanings the word *believe* can convey:

But to as many as did receive and welcome Him, He gave the authority (power, privilege, right) to become the children of God, that is, to those who believe in (ADHERE TO, TRUST IN AND RELY ON) His name.
                    Emphasis Added

When you believe God, you adhere to His teachings, you trust what He says, and you rely on Him—just like a small child. You instinctively know that God, your heavenly Father, is totally trustworthy and totally reliable. That is what it means to have faith in God.

WHAT, THEN, IS UNBELIEF?

Unbelief is the absence of trust in God and, as such, is the greatest insult we could ever pay Him. When we have no faith in God, we are saying: "God, I don't believe You. I cannot trust Your Word. I cannot rely on what You say."

Calling someone a liar is an insult in any part of the world—even in cultures where lying is condoned and expected in certain circumstances. Anyone has to think twice before calling someone a liar, for this is serious business. And how can we expect to receive God's favor when we insult Him with our lack of trust in His integrity?

Adam and Eve did not fall from their original exalted state because of some sexual misconduct, as some have imagined. God created them for each other's pleasure, as well as for His own fellowship. They fell because they did not believe what God told them. Their fateful sin was the simple failure to believe. This is what the Bible calls *"unbelief."*

God set certain boundaries for Adam and Eve and told them that if they crossed those boundaries, they would die. He wasn't trying to limit their fun in life or withhold something meaningful from them. It was just a test of their faith. Would the first man and woman whom God had created for fellowship believe what He was telling them?

Adam and Eve seemed to believe God—until Satan interfered and deceived them. But even Satan was part of God's plan. God had to permit this enemy to exist in order to present an alternative to the truth. If we had no choice but to believe God, that wouldn't be faith. Satan created an alternative to the word of the Creator, to see if Adam and Eve would still believe Him.

Satan laughed at God's words—as he still does. He assured Adam and Eve that what God had said was not true, that they would not die if they disobeyed God. In fact, he said, the opposite was true. They would actually become like God:

> *You will become just like God, knowing everything, both good and evil.*   Genesis 3:5

It Is Somehow Easier to Believe a Lie

Has it always been easier for men and women to believe a lie than to believe the truth? Since the fall of man in the Garden, since man has a fallen nature, and since the world is now filled with darkness, a lie often sounds more plausible than the truth. But was it always so? Would this have been true in Adam's day?

God could have appeared to Adam and Eve that day and argued His point or debated His case, but He doesn't do it that way. He speaks, and then He waits to see if we will believe Him or if we, like Adam before us, will prefer to believe a lie. Those who believe God are known as men and women of faith, and those who do not believe Him are known as *"unbelievers."* And there is a great gulf fixed between the two:

> *Don't team up with those who are unbelievers. How can goodness be a partner with wickedness? How can light live with darkness?*   2 Corinthians 6:14

Unbelievers *are automatically linked to* wickedness *and* darkness.

HOW CAN WE BELIEVE?

"How can we believe in a God we cannot see?" some would ask. "How can we *not* believe?" I would answer. As the Scriptures declare, *"God is not a man that He should lie"*:

> *God is not a man, that he should lie.*
> *He is not a human, that he should change his mind.*
> *Has he ever spoken and failed to act?*
> *Has he ever promised and not carried it through?*
> *I received a command to bless; he has blessed, and I cannot reverse it!*
>
> Numbers 23:19-20

"Just believe Me, and you will prosper or be delivered from danger!"

"Just believe Me, and you will be saved," God says to the sinner. "Just believe Me, and you will be healed," He says to the Christian. "Just believe Me, and you will prosper or be delivered from danger." That is His promise. "Just believe." "Trust Me." "Rely on My words." That's what faith is all about.

I like to call Christians *"believers,"* and the Bible also uses that phrase:

I CAN DO THIS!

Don't let anyone think less of you because you are young. Be an example to all believers in what you teach, in the way you live, in your love, your faith, and your purity. 1 Timothy 4:12

There are, of course, degrees of believing. We have little-believing believers, average-believing believers, more-believing believers and most-believing believers. But since everything we receive from God comes by way of faith, it behooves us all to get more of this mysterious and powerful element known as faith and to be sure that our faith pleases God.

HOW DO YOU GET FAITH?

Faith is received in two ways. First, it is a gift from God, and every person alive has an element of it:

God hath dealt to every man the measure of faith.
Romans 12:3, KJV

Some have received more than just elementary faith and seem to have an unusual potential for believing the supernatural. But all of us can grow in faith, for it is also learned:

Faith comes from listening to this message of good news—the Good News about Christ. Romans 10:17

The King James Version says it this way:

So then faith cometh by hearing, and hearing by the word of God. Romans 10:17

Not only can our faith grow, but God has declared that He wants to take us *"from faith to faith"*:

For therein is the righteousness of God revealed from faith to faith. Romans 1:17, KJV

How Can Our Faith Grow?

And how can our faith grow? It can grow, first, by deepening our relationship with God. The better we know Him, the more we realize what He can do for us and how easily He can do it.

Secondly, our faith grows by allowing God to work on our behalf. If He has done something for us once, we have no problem believing that He will do it again.

In a similar way, our faith grows by hearing what God has done for others. Because He *"doesn't show partiality"* (Acts 10:34), or, as the King James Version puts it, He *"is no respecter of persons,"* we can be assured that what He has done for someone else He can and will also do for us.

Because both faith and unbelief are learned, they are also both contagious. You can catch faith from others, and others can catch it from you. Therefore if you spend too much time with doubters, their doubts will begin to rub off on you.

Finally, faith grows by learning God's ways and learning God's Word: *"faith comes by hearing"* (NKJ). When you fill your mind and heart with God's thoughts and God's words, it's easy to believe that He can do anything, and that nothing is *"too hard for the Lord"* (Genesis 18:14).

The biblical definition of faith, *"the confident assurance that what we hope for is going to happen, ... the evidence of things we cannot yet see"* or, as the King James Version expresses it, *"the substance of things hoped for, the evidence of things not seen,"* shows us the power of faith. It makes real what seems to be unreal. It makes possible what seems to be impossible. Indeed, *"anything is possible if a person believes."*

When we have faith in God, therefore, we don't need anything else. Faith is *"substance (confident assurance)."* Faith is *"evidence."* What more could we possibly need? With faith in God, each of us can say with certainty, *"I Can Do This!"*

> **Doubt and unbelief are always accompanied by disobedience, just as faith is always accompanied by obedience!**

FAITH IS ALWAYS ACCOMPANIED BY OBEDIENCE

There is another very important element of faith which we often ignore. It is obedience. Faith and obedience go hand in hand, and they cannot be separated. You cannot believe and disobey. If you genuinely believe, you *will* obey. Adam and Eve grew to doubt God's words, and it was this doubt that led to their disobedience.

Sinners don't believe in Hell—even if they insist that they do. If they really believed in Hell, they would waste no time in getting right with God to avoid any possibility of going to such an awful place.

Faith and obedience are inseparable. In his letter to the churches, James taught forcefully:

It isn't enough just to have faith. Faith that doesn't show itself by good deeds is no faith at all—it is dead and useless. James 2:17

Even so faith, if it hath not works, is dead, being alone. KJV

Fool! When will you ever learn that faith that does not result in good deeds is useless? James 2:20

But do you want to know, O foolish man, that faith without works is dead? NKJ

Just as the body is dead without a spirit, so also faith is dead without good deeds. James 2:26

For as the body without the spirit is dead, so faith without works is dead also. NKJ

Doubt and unbelief are always accompanied by disobedience, just as faith is always accompanied by obedience. We see it in every Bible story. In the case of the heroes of faith, they believed, and because they believed, they obeyed.

Abel believed God, so he offered the sacrifice God said was necessary. Cain doubted its importance, so he disobeyed and lost favor with God.

Noah believed God that a flood was coming, so he built an ark. Those who didn't believe refused to get aboard the ark, and they all drowned.

UNBELIEF IS
THE GREATEST OF SINS

Unbelief is the greatest of sins. Adultery is not the worst sin, although it does great damage to the family, and God condemns it. Even blasphemy against God is not the worst sin. Each of us, as individuals, might have a particular sin that we consider to be worse than others, but God says that the worst sin, in His eyes, is unbelief. And since His is the only opinion that counts in this matter, unbelief wins the contest. If God says it's the worst sin, then it's definitely the worst.

It was unbelief (and only unbelief) that caused certain of God's chosen people to be severed from His blessings:

Remember — those branches, the Jews, were broken off because they didn't believe God, and you are there because you do believe.   Romans 11:20

Because of unbelief they were broken off, and you stand
by faith. NKJ

FAITH IS THE ONE REQUIREMENT FOR SALVATION

Just as unbelief is the greatest of sins, belief (faith) is
the one requirement for salvation. When the Philippian
jailer asked Paul and Silas, *"Sirs, what must I do to be*
saved?" (Acts 16:30), their response was, *"BELIEVE on the*
Lord Jesus and you will be saved, along with your entire
household" (Verse 31, Emphasis Added).

Believe! Have faith in God! Faith opens every door.
Jesus said:

Anything is possible if a person believes.
Mark 9:23

The King James Version uses these powerful words:

All things are possible to him that believeth.

ALL THINGS!
ALL THINGS ARE POSSIBLE!

All things are possible if we can only develop simple
faith.

And, again, as Paul wrote:

I can do everything with the help of Christ who gives
me the strength I need. Philippians 4:13

What can you and I do if we trust in God? ALL THINGS, EVERYTHING, ANYTHING. Since this is true, you can overcome the seemingly impossible situations of your life today. Say it with me, and say it with faith: *"I Can Do This!"*

Now, go out and do it in Jesus' name.

CHAPTER 2

WHAT DO I NEED TO LEARN?

It was by faith that Abraham obeyed when God called him to leave home and go to another land that God would give him as his inheritance. He went without knowing where he was going. Hebrews 11:8

We all have a lot to learn about faith, and who better than Abraham to teach us simple faith? He was, after all, the father of faith. From his life, we see some of the important elements that need to be learned in order to please God.

AN INTIMATE RELATIONSHIP

The first necessary element in simple faith is an intimate relationship with God. Abraham knew Him well and so he knew when God was speaking to him. The better you know God the more you can trust Him. The closer you walk with Him, the more confidence you have in His Word.

Your faith is not only in God, but also in your relationship with Him. If you know Him as Father, you are aware that He loves you; He is concerned about your welfare; He is looking out for you; He will never fail you; He knows what is best for you; and He will not let anything hurt you.

Even earthly fathers are generally concerned about giving good things to their children. Jesus said:

If you sinful people know how to give good gifts to your children, how much more will your heavenly Father give ... to those who ask him.   Luke 11:13

Faith cannot work without this element of personal relationship, for without it you have no rights. You are a stranger. You are outside the covenant. You are not part of the family.

When you have a personal relationship with God, everything changes. You know that your Father will take care of you and that all of His promises are yours to claim and enjoy.

Do you want to have greater faith, so that you can overcome the things life throws at you periodically? Then get closer to God, for the relationship produces the faith.

HEARING THE VOICE OF GOD

Let's look at our text for this chapter again:

By faith Abraham, WHEN HE WAS CALLED to go out into a place which he should after receive for an inheritance, obeyed; and he went out, not knowing whither he went. Hebrews 11:8, KJV, Emphasis Added

The second important element of simple faith is hearing the voice of God. Jesus said: *"Have faith in God"* (Mark 11:22). He didn't say, "Have faith in yourself, have faith in the Church or have faith in some prominent Christian leader." Faith is believing what God tells you, and how can He tell you anything if you have no relationship with Him and have not grown accustomed to hearing His voice?

Faith cannot work without this element of personal relationship!

Believing for something you want is vain—unless you have a relationship with God and unless He has shown you that what you are asking for is His will for you. Memorizing Bible verses and declaring them is useless—if you don't know God and understand what He wants for your life. Praying in faith in the name of Jesus is also useless—if you don't know Him and have not yet received the authority to use His name.

When the sons of Sceva saw Paul casting out devils, it seemed so easy that they tried it themselves. They used all the right words, but they had no authority, so it didn't work for them as it had for Paul. One of the devils responded: *"I know Jesus, and I know Paul. But who are you?"* (Acts 19:15). Then the devils jumped on the men, beat them up, and sent them running for their lives.

First comes the intimate relationship with God, and then we must hear His voice.

There is a step beyond this. When you have known the Lord for some time, and you are walking close to Him, His thoughts actually become your thoughts. His heart becomes your heart. It is then that you can do as the Scriptures suggest, *"ask any request you like"*:

> But if you stay joined to me and my words remain in you, you may ask any request you like, and it will be granted!   John 15:7

It is only then that God will grant you *"your heart's desires"*:

> Take delight in the LORD,
> and he will give you your heart's desires.
> Commit everything you do to the LORD.
> Trust him, and he will help you.   Psalm 37:4-5

These promises are not for the carnal or worldly. They're for those who are walking close to the Lord, those who are hearing His voice and feeling His heart.

Many people are exercising faith for things that are not God's will, things that don't please Him and cannot bring Him glory. Please don't be guilty of wasting your time on such pursuits. Know God's will and believe for that which emanates from His heart, and you will have answers to your prayers.

Thank God that He doesn't hear every prayer. Thank God that He doesn't respond to every whim. When we ask and believe for things that are not good for us, He must, in His mercy and great love for us, decline.

We don't give our children everything they ask for. If we gave them something they were not able to handle properly, they could hurt themselves or they could hurt other people. When we truly love our children, we give them what we know to be good for them. If they're angry and pout for a while when they're denied something we deem damaging to their well being, we're sorry, but we just cannot give them dangerous things. We love them too much to do that.

We are much wiser than our children. We know better than they do what is good for them, and so we withhold from them things that could be harmful. Could God do any less for His children? He said:

And even when you do ask, you don't get it because your whole motive is wrong—you want only what will give you pleasure.   James 4:3

Faith is not what you want—unless what you want corresponds with what God wants for you, and He has no obligation to respond to you when you *"ask amiss"* (KJV). Many people act in faith and get themselves in the worst kind of trouble. God has promised to be with us, to help us in every situation of life, to provide our every need and to protect us from every enemy—when we hear His voice and move at His command. He is not obligated to provide the things we desire—unless we are using them for His glory.

> **The various ministries of the Church are ordained by God, and He sets them in the Church in the manner that pleases Him!**

Abraham went out of Ur because he was called by God to go out. God doesn't promise to bless all *our* ideas, all *our* plans. When we act on *His* ideas and *His* plans, then He blesses. Therefore, we must wait for Him to speak, and when He speaks, we can then act on what He has said. We don't conjure up a vision and then ask God to bless it. We wait for His vision and know that He will bless it and bring the fulfillment of it.

Even in the exercise of the gifts of the Spirit, we don't act on our own. The gifts of the Spirit belong to the Spirit, and He distributes them *"as He wills"* (KJV):

It is the one and only Holy Spirit who distributes these gifts. He alone decides which gift each person should have.

1 Corinthians 12:11

The gifts of the Spirit work at His command and for the purposes He decrees.

Likewise, the various ministries of the Church are ordained by God, and He sets them in the Church in the manner that pleases Him:

Here is a list of some of the members that God has placed in the body of Christ:
first are apostles,
second are prophets,
third are teachers,
then those who do miracles,
those who have the gift of healing,
those who can help others,
those who can get others to work together,
those who speak in unknown languages.

1 Corinthians 12:28

Who placed them? God. And so they are His, and they are to serve His purposes. Ministers at every level are to function as God desires and for the goals He has in mind. This is the reason that carnal Christians cannot exercise faith. They would exercise it for carnal ends, and their loving heavenly Father cannot permit that. Thank God!

Hear God's voice, get His mind, feel His heart, find His will, and then faith will work for you too. This second element of the successful life of simple faith—hearing the voice of God—has no substitute.

That Word Obedience Again

We looked briefly at this matter of obedience in Chapter 1, but it deserves more of our attention. Again, our text for this chapter says:

It was by faith that Abraham obeyed when God called him to leave home and go to another land that God would give him as his inheritance. He went without knowing where he was going.   Hebrews 11:8

The third important element of simple faith is obedience. Faith demands obedient action. Abraham went out. Noah built the ark. Abel offered the proper sacrifice. Gideon called the men of Israel to battle. Deborah accompanied her general to the front.

As we noted earlier, faith without works is dead, and it is therefore a false faith. If you believe, you obey. If you were not sure that what God said was true, you would not bother to build an ark. You would wait to see if it was really going to rain or not. If you were not sure you had heard from God, you would not start a journey across the desert. You would wait to see if anyone else confirmed the existence of a city *"whose builder and maker is God"* (Hebrews 11:10, KJV). If you were not sure of God's will, you would not make a proper sacrifice, and you would not call the nation to battle. You would wait to see what others did.

"Believing" without action, without doing, without obeying, is really a lie. That type of faith is empty, vain, and useless. It is false faith, nothing more than empty words. All the heroes of faith became heroes because they acted upon their faith, for faith demands action.

"When he was called ... obeyed" (KJV) portrays the sense that Abraham did not waste time thinking about it, meditating on it or praying about it. He simply obeyed.

Abraham obeyed when he was called, and we must learn to obey when God speaks to us as well. Next year may be too late, next month may be too late, next week may be too late, and even tomorrow may be too late. Obey when you are called. Do what God is bidding you to do now.

If God tells you to do something "tomorrow," then that's different. Obey when you are called. If it's tomorrow, then that's the time to obey, and if it's for next year, then that's the time to obey. But if it's for the here and now, then tomorrow or next year won't do.

How many others were called to build a holy nation? Perhaps many, but it was Abraham who arrived in Canaan ready to do God's will. He got there despite every obstacle, despite everything his neighbors and family and friends said or did, and despite the enemies that threatened him along the way. Abraham got there because he believed God, and when you believe, nothing can stop you. You and God make a majority, and that's why *"all things are possible"* to you and you *"can do all things through Christ."*

Many start out well, but they later drop out somewhere along the way. Obedience, however, is not for a moment, an hour, a day, a week or a month. Faith causes you to keep going until you get there, and complete faith brings about complete obedience. The Scriptures state very simply and yet clearly:

I Can Do This!

*And they went forth to go into the land of Canaan; and
INTO THE LAND OF CANAAN THEY CAME.*
Genesis 12:5, KJV, Emphasis Added

That's real faith! It not only starts; it finishes.

Not Knowing

Again, our text:

*By faith Abraham, when he was called to go out into a
place which he should after receive for an inheritance,
obeyed; and he went out, NOT KNOWING whither he
went.*　　　Hebrews 11:8, KJV, Emphasis Added

The fourth important element of simple faith is the
very nature of faith—*"not knowing,"* not seeing. Faith is
not what you see; it is what you don't see. It is not what
you have; it is what you don't have. It's not what you
have evidence of already; it is what you know is coming.
Faith itself is *"the evidence of things not seen,"* and that
should be enough. You don't need to see or know or have
any other evidence. The evidence of faith is enough.

You don't need to see the city made without hands.
You know it's there, because God said it was. You don't
need to see the first drops of rain. You can start building
an ark on dry ground, because God said you would need
it to save your family from the coming flood. You don't
need to learn human warfare tactics before you call the

38

men of the nation to battle. God said you were a mighty man of valor, and you're sure that He will give you the victory. His word is evidence enough for you, so you command the trumpets to be blown—by faith.

Hesitant faith is failing faith. Living faith acts without delay. So not knowing, not seeing, not having any other evidence of what God has said must never deter you or delay you.

If you have totally logical reasons for acting, you may not be moving in faith at all. If every sign is in your favor, you may be making a big mistake. In fact, it is a common thing to mistake favorable circumstances, wonderful opportunities or the goodwill of people as being God's way of speaking to us. What you are contemplating may indeed be the will of God, but favorable circumstances or favorable opinions don't necessarily make it so.

> *Faith is not what you see; it is what you don't see!*

When God speaks to us to do something, there is often nothing visible upon which to base our actions. It may seem not to be an opportune time. It may seem that everything is against us. But if we are to fulfill God's purposes in our lives, we must act by faith, for faith is evidence enough. We don't need to see favorable circumstances or to know of any favorable opinions.

Abraham forsook his homeland and began a long journey without knowing exactly where he was going. He didn't have a road map detailing every part of the trip. He didn't know exactly where the Promised Land was located. He didn't know how long it would take to get there. He went out, *NOT KNOWING*.

Faith may include: not knowing WHY, not knowing WHO, not knowing WHEN, not knowing HOW and not knowing WHICH WAY. When we already know everything, we don't need faith. It doesn't take faith to follow a road map. If you already know who will accompany you and who will support you and which way you will turn and every other detail, you're no longer walking by faith.

Paul wrote to the churches:

Now that we are saved, we eagerly look forward to this freedom. For if you already have something, you don't need to hope for it. But if we look forward to something we don't have yet, we must wait patiently and confidently. Romans 8:24-25

We do not look at the things which are seen, but at the things which are not seen. For the things which are seen are temporary, but the things which are not seen are eternal. 2 Corinthians 4:18, NKJ

Indeed, this is part of the critical foundation of this teaching:

What is faith? ... It is the evidence of things we cannot yet see. Hebrews 11:1

Faith is the substance of THINGS HOPED FOR, the evidence of THINGS NOT SEEN.

KJV, Emphasis Added

In the life of faith, we don't fix our minds on a certain course; we open ourselves to God's course. We don't insist on a certain companion; we open ourselves to God's choice. We don't concentrate on one source of supply; we are open to God's endless variety of sources. We become willing to begin the journey, not knowing the how, the when, the where and the who. We know God, and that's enough.

PERSEVERANCE

And even when he reached the land God promised him, he lived there by faith—for he was like a foreigner, living in a tent. And so did Isaac and Jacob, to whom God gave the same promise. Abraham did this because he was confidently looking forward to a city with eternal foundations, a city designed and built by God.

Hebrews 11:9-10

The final element in simple faith is perseverance. Too many people are easily discouraged when they don't see God's promises fulfilled today or tomorrow. It took time for Abraham to reach Canaan, and it took determination for him to keep moving toward that final goal. Any steps backward or any unnecessary detours would surely have prolonged the realization of God's promises for his life.

Getting to the Promised Land required traveling across deserts and hostile territory, but whatever he happened to face along the way, Abraham was determined to persevere and to reach his place of fulfilled destiny.

> *Whatever he happened to face along the way, Abraham was determined to persevere and to reach his place of fulfilled destiny!*

And there are always personal considerations. We know nothing, for example, about the attitude of Abraham's parents to all of this. It would not have been unusual for them to have been alarmed at the prospect of his leaving home and security to reach what to them must have seemed like some vague goal.

We know little or nothing about the attitude of Sarah at the time. Did she understand what Abraham was doing? Did she question him regularly, "Where is that city you told me about?" That would not have been unusual. Our walk with God is often complicated by our personal circumstances.

Nothing is said in the biblical account concerning these personal matters. Nothing is said about them because, in the end, they could not be allowed to influence the outcome. Abraham couldn't allow what his parents thought or said to hold him back. He couldn't be deterred by the fact that his wife might disagree. He must reach the Promised Land. He must obey God, for he believed, and faith demands action—whatever others happen to think at the moment.

We can only imagine the thoughts that went through Abraham's mind as he traversed the desert, step by step, facing the daily struggles of obedience. What is clear is that he and Sarah *were* tempted to return to their former home:

And truly if they had called to mind that country from which they had come out, they would have had opportunity to return. But now they desire a better, that is, a heavenly country. Therefore God is not ashamed to be called their God, for He has prepared a city for them.
Hebrews 11:15-16, NKJ

"They would have had opportunity," or as the King James Version says it, *"They might have had opportunity,"* but they didn't entertain the thought. They refused to give Satan a place in their thinking. They refused to allow circumstances to defeat them. By keeping their eyes focused on the goal, they were able to move forward toward the promise of God. There is no substitute for perseverance.

FAITH IS ALWAYS TESTED

And even when he reached the land God promised him, he lived there by faith—for he was like a foreigner, liv-

ing in a tent. And so did Isaac and Jacob, to whom God gave the same promise. Abraham did this because he was confidently looking forward to a city with eternal foundations, a city designed and built by God.

Hebrews 11:9-10

We must not be surprised that Canaan was not attained in a day. Faith must be tried to see if it is true faith. The Scriptures declare it to be so:

These trials are only to test your faith, to show that it is strong and pure. It is being tested as fire tests and purifies gold—and your faith is far more precious to God than mere gold. So if your faith remains strong after being tried by fiery trials, it will bring you much praise and glory and honor on the day when Jesus Christ is revealed to the whole world. 1 Peter 1:7

God has the right to test us, and much of what comes our way—temptation, persecution, delay, hardship and suffering—is nothing more than that: a test of our faith, a test of our willingness, a test of our perseverance. If we are determined to persevere, nothing can stop us, and nothing can hold us back. There are not enough demons in Hell to prevent us from accomplishing the will of God—if we make up our minds to persevere no matter what comes our way.

Each day Abraham had to take a new step of faith, so each day he had to get new direction from God. Each day he had to make decisions that would affect his future, the future of his family, and the future of the nation he was called to build. Those could not have been easy steps to take, and they could not have been easy decisions for this man of faith. Abraham, however, was determined to obey God. God had spoken to him, and he must not fail. He kept going, and thus passed every test of his faith.

Victorious Faith

Thus, step by step—by faith—Abraham arrived in the Promised Land. Simple faith will always bring victory to those who possess it. Simple faith is never denied by our heavenly Father.

But, as we have noted, when Abraham arrived in Canaan, his journey was not yet ended. Laying hold of what God had promised him would require that he live long years as a foreigner in tents. He was also willing to do this. Indeed, he was willing to do whatever was necessary. He had been willing to leave the security of his home, his family and a well-developed city because he considered God's word to be greater security than any of them, and that's what faith is all about.

So, if Abraham could go forth into the unknown, with all of its challenges, to begin a new life, then you, too, can use your faith in God to overcome the impossible situations life throws at you today. Say it with me, and say it with faith: *"I Can Do This!"*

Now, go out and do it in Jesus' name.

PART II

LEARNING FROM THE HEROES OF FAITH

CHAPTER 3

ABEL: BRINGING A MORE ACCEPTABLE SACRIFICE

It was by faith that Abel brought a more acceptable offering to God than Cain did. God accepted Abel's offering to show that he was a righteous man. And although Abel is long dead, he still speaks to us because of his faith.   Hebrews 11:4

We looked at Abraham first to lay some necessary groundwork for the subject of faith, but the first hero of faith listed in Hebrews 11 was not a conquering warrior. Rather, he was a dead man, slain in a fit of jealousy by his own brother. Abel's story, however, is worth telling, not only because he was of the first generation born on the Earth, the inheritors of the faith delivered by God to his parents, Adam and Eve, but also because *"he still speaks to us."* Think about that. Abel still has a voice, although he has been dead now for thousands of years.

WHAT CAUSED CAIN TO HATE ABEL?

> *Our God is a just God, and He does not accept one man and reject another without good reason!*

When looking at Abel, it's always necessary to look at Cain, as well, for Cain was the opposite of his brother. This is one of the reasons he hated his brother so much and, in the end, killed him. What was it that infuriated Cain so much? Genesis captures the essence of Abel's life in a few short verses:

When they [Cain and Abel] grew up, Abel became a shepherd, while Cain was a farmer. At harvest time Cain brought to the LORD a gift of his farm produce, while Abel brought several choice lambs from the best of his flock. The LORD accepted Abel and his offering, but he did not accept Cain and his offering. This made Cain very angry and dejected.

Genesis 4:2-5

It was the favor of God upon Abel that angered Cain,

ABEL: BRINGING A MORE ACCEPTABLE SACRIFICE

and the favor of God upon Abel was a result of his obedience to the Lord's commands. Hebrews states: *"Abel offered unto God a more excellent sacrifice than Cain"* (KJV) and Genesis says: *"And the LORD had respect unto Abel and to his offering: but unto Cain and to his offering he had not respect"* (KJV). We have to ask why.

WHAT WAS IT THAT SET ABEL APART?

Our God is a just God, and He does not accept one man and reject another without good reason. He is merciful. *"If thou doest well,"* He told Cain, *"shalt thou not be accepted?"* (Verse 7, KJV). God blessed Abel because he did well, and He could not bless Cain because he did not do well. It's as simple as that.

If Abel was aware that he was doing well, and Cain was aware that he was not doing well, at some point and in some way, God must have made it clear to the both of them exactly what He expected of them. Probably Adam and Eve, taught by the Lord to make animal sacrifices for their sins, had, in turn, taught their sons what God considered to be an acceptable sacrifice.

Abel believed and obeyed, bringing *"the firstlings of his flock and of the fat thereof"* (KJV). Cain, however, refused and brought, instead, *"the fruit of the ground"* (KJV). That sounds like a rebellious spirit to me.

WHY DID CAIN REBEL?

This whole situation was complicated by the sibling

rivalry that Cain felt for his brother and by the fact that Abel was a shepherd, while Cain was a farmer. Cain was proud of his produce, and there's nothing wrong with that. His failure came when he refused to believe that a sacrifice to God had to be a blood sacrifice. His vegetables were just as good as Abel's lambs, he reasoned. Why should he offer a lamb? God, however, declared Cain's sacrifice to be unacceptable.

God is not a capricious God, and Cain's act was not a simple case of ignorance or misunderstanding. Cain hated his brother, for light and darkness can never mix, and the one dispels the other.

The blessing of God was upon Abel's life, and it was not upon Cain's life. Cain was a sinner. When reproving him, God said: *"sin lies at the door"* (NKJ). Cain had chosen the life of sin, so he had placed himself at odds with God Almighty.

What Cain did, when his sacrifice was rejected by God, reveals the sad state of his soul. He rose up in anger and jealousy and killed his brother. How sad!

What had Abel done to him? Had he caused Cain's shame? No, Cain had brought shame upon himself. Had Abel humiliated his brother? No, Cain had humiliated himself.

Cain was not really angry with Abel; he was angry with God. When he raised his hand against Abel, he was actually raising his hand against God.

But there was surely more to the story than this. Abel must have warned his brother not to displease God and, he, therefore became a thorn under Cain's skin. If Abel were somehow removed, Cain reasoned, things would surely go better for him.

WHAT WAS CAIN'S SAD END?

The story of Cain and Abel is a sad one, not only because the first child born in this world rebelled against God and became a murderer, but also because the punishment Cain suffered, as a result of his sin, was so great. Unbelief has terrible consequences. God cannot bless those who refuse to believe Him. Cain, in fact, felt that his punishment was more than he could bear:

And Cain said to the Lord, "My punishment is greater than I can bear! Surely You have driven me out this day from the face of the ground; I shall be hidden from Your face; I shall be a fugitive and a vagabond on the earth, and it will happen that anyone who finds me will kill me." Genesis 4:13-14, NKJ

This story ends with the ominous words:

Cain went out from the presence of the Lord.
Genesis 4:16, KJV

What could be more sad? Killing Abel did not bring him the relief he sought. It only made things worse, much worse.

JESUS REMEMBERED ABEL

Jesus remembered Abel and called him *"righteous"* (Matthew 23:35). Let us learn from this first-generation

53

son of the Earth the importance of believing what God says and acting upon it.

If Abel could overcome in his day, then you, too, can face the seemingly impossible situations of your daily life. Say with me right now ,and say it with faith, *"I Can Do This!"*

Now, go out and do it in Jesus' name.

CHAPTER 4

ENOCH: BEING TAKEN UP TO HEAVEN

It was by faith that Enoch was taken up to heaven without dying—"suddenly he disappeared because God took him." But before he was taken up, he was approved as pleasing to God.   Hebrews 11:5

Of all the Bible characters, only two were *"taken up to heaven without dying"* or as the King James Version calls this strange occurrence, being *"translated."* Enoch and Elijah are unique in Bible history, and the reason for Enoch's unique experience was his *"testimony"* (KJV). He *"was approved as pleasing to God."*

WHAT WAS ENOCH'S TESTIMONY?

Genesis confirms and expands on Enoch's *"testimony"*:

When Enoch was 65 years old, his son Methuselah was born. After the birth of Methuselah, Enoch lived another 300 years in close fellowship with God, and he had other sons and daughters. Enoch lived 365 years in all. He enjoyed a close relationship with God throughout his life. Then suddenly, he disappeared because God took him.   Genesis 5:21-24

Enoch *"walked with God"* (KJV) or *"lived ... in close fellowship with God."* He had a personal relationship with God, one that was called *"close"* and one that continued *"throughout his life."* He loved God, and when you love someone, you trust them, you believe them, and you want to be with them. He so wanted to be with God that God just took him.

While he was here, Enoch's love and trust *"pleased God,"* and everybody knew it. This is why he had such a powerful *"testimony."*

A testimony is more than words; it's your life. People around you know if God's blessings are upon you or not. They sense it when what you do finds favor with the Almighty.

Amazingly, the Old Testament has nothing more to say about Enoch. He *"walked with God,"* he *"pleased God,"* and he had a good *"testimony."* But what else needs to be said? What greater legacy could any man have left for his children? What greater example could he have given to his neighbors and friends? What greater lesson could he have taught those of us who study his life? Enoch was a man of simple faith.

ENOCH PROPHESIED

The New Testament does have something more to say of Enoch. It says that he *"prophesied"*:

> *Now Enoch, who lived seven generations after Adam, prophesied about these people. He said,*
>
> *"Look, the Lord is coming with thousands of his holy ones. He will bring the people of the world to judgment. He will convict the ungodly of all the evil things they have done in rebellion and of all the insults that godless sinners have spoken against him."*
>
> Jude 14-15

> **Enoch had a personal relationship with God, one that was called "close" and one that continued "throughout his life!"**

Enoch not only believed what God was showing him; he spoke it out in prophecy to others. He could not have understood all that he was saying, since his words were for a future time. Still, he was willing to speak it anyway—whether he understood it or not.

Since the prophecy that Enoch gave was for a future time, it did not come to pass during his lifetime. But when God shows us something, we can bank on it. His word never fails. He will come *"with ten thousands of His saints"* (KJV). You can count on that fact. Enoch was sure of it, and you can be too.

Enoch Was Translated

God was pleased with Enoch and gave him a unique reward for his faith, taking him out of this world by an unusual means. He was *"translated,"* meaning that he did not experience death, but, instead, was physically taken up by God alive into Heaven. Enoch must have gotten so close to God that he was too good for this world. There is no other explanation for this amazing phenomenon.

What were the circumstances of Enoch's daily life? We don't know exactly. Did he own a big house? Was it located in a good part of town? Did he have a good credit rating? Did his business prosper? Did his wife treat him well? Did his children respect him? None of these questions are answered in Sacred Writ. What we do know is that one moment he was here, and the next moment he was gone—because he *"walked with God"* and *"had a testimony that he pleased God."* So the circumstances of his life didn't really matter then, and they still don't matter today. Enoch *"pleased God"*—whatever the circumstances of his life, and each of us must learn this valuable lesson.

If Enoch could overcome so wonderfully despite the

impossible circumstances of his daily life (and you can be sure they existed), then you can overcome too. Say with me today, and say it with faith, *"I Can Do This!"*

Now, go out and do it in Jesus' name.

CHAPTER 5

NOAH: BUILDING AN ARK AND PREACHING RIGHTEOUSNESS

It was by faith that Noah built an ark to save his family from the flood. He obeyed God, who warned him about something that had never happened before. By his faith he condemned the rest of the world and was made right in God's sight. Hebrews 11:7

Noah was *"warned"* by God *"about something that had never happened before."* This shows that he loved God, he walked with God, he listened to God's voice, and when God spoke to him, he believed what God was saying. Because of that, the Bible calls him *"a just man"* who was *"perfect in his generations"* (Genesis 6:9, KJV). There was a reason for these words.

You can't be *"warned of God"* (KJV) if you're not hear-

I CAN DO THIS!

ing from Him. God desires to speak to every one of us, but He can only speak to those who are willing to listen. Noah had come to know the voice of God by walking with Him and listening to Him on a regular basis. That set him apart.

> It's possible that Noah learned his faith from his father, Lamech, for Lamech foresaw blessing in his son!

DID NOAH LEARN FROM HIS FATHER?

It's possible that Noah learned his faith from his father, Lamech, for Lamech foresaw blessing in his son (see Genesis 5:28-29). Whatever the source of his religious training, Noah developed into a man of simple faith who was warned by God *"of things not seen as yet"* (KJV). In other words, one day God showed Noah something that no one else on the face of the Earth knew about. He showed His servant that something would happen that had never happened before.

When God created the Earth, He created an efficient system for watering the land. It was not rain, as we know it today. Rain is destructive, for through rain we either get too much water or too little water. Too much rain washes away the topsoil and the nutrients in the soil, and when a

62

hard rain is over, it leaves stones sticking out from the surface of the ground. God had a better system. He would water the Earth from *"fountains of the deep"*:

In the six hundredth year of Noah's life, in the second month, the seventeenth day of the month, the same day were all THE FOUNTAINS OF THE great DEEP broken up, and the windows of heaven were opened. Genesis 7:11, KJV, Emphasis Added

God's creation had grown increasingly sinful, until He was actually sorry He had ever made man and felt compelled to judge him. He would do this through a great flood. The fountains of the deep would be *"broken up,"* and torrents of water would begin falling from the sky. It you had never seen such a thing or never heard of its existence, would you believe it could happen? Probably not.

I've found it very interesting to watch those who have never seen snow before. When they see those magical flakes of frozen beauty drifting downward and slowly covering everything in their path, they get very excited. They're both terrified and happy at the same time, and they laugh and cry all at once. You may think that's odd, but if you had never seen snow, you don't know how you might react to seeing it for the first time.

Noah heard the voice of God, and God said it was going to rain and that Noah must prepare a great boat in order to save his family. Although no one else wanted to believe it, Noah did believe it and began to get ready and to warn others to get ready. Because of this, Peter later called him *"a preacher of righteousness"* (2 Peter 2:5, KJV).

WHAT MOVED NOAH TO BUILD THE ARK?

The writer of Hebrews states that Noah built the ark because he was *"moved with fear"* (KJV). Faith gives us a healthy fear. I call it a "holy" fear. Parents need to instill a certain fear in their children—a fear of knowing the consequences of disobedience. And, as believers in Christ, we need that same healthy fear of God and of His words. The Scriptures declare:

THE FEAR OF THE LORD is the beginning of wisdom.   Psalm 111:10, KJV, Emphasis Added

FEAR OF THE LORD lengthens one's life, but the years of the wicked are cut short.
Proverbs 10:27, Emphasis Added

By humility and THE FEAR OF THE LORD are riches, and honour, and life.
Proverbs 22:4, KJV, Emphasis Added

In THE FEAR OF THE LORD is strong confidence.
Proverbs 14:26, KJV, Emphasis Added

THE FEAR OF THE LORD is a fountain of life.
Proverbs 14:27, KJV, Emphasis Added

NOAH WAS MOVED TO ACTION

A holy fear moved Noah to action, and he *"built an ark."* He felt compelled to build it because he believed what God had said. In this way, Noah was obedient to God. His faith compelled him to act:

> *So Noah did everything exactly as God had commanded him.* Genesis 6:22

> *So Noah did exactly as the LORD had commanded him.* Genesis 7:5

What powerful words! No wonder Noah was one of the greatest men of all times! He *"did exactly as the LORD commanded him."* That's faith!

THE LONG DELAY

When nearly one hundred and twenty years had passed, and still the rain God had spoken to him about had not yet come, Noah's faith still did not waver. He continued building and preaching.

Imagine the mocking of the people around him. They would have been sure that old Noah had completely "flipped his lid," and they were not about to believe his preaching or to get into that ugly box he had made on dry land. What made him believe that thing would even float? But Noah was not deterred by the negative reaction of his neighbors, and he kept right on preparing for what he was sure was to come.

Noah Said What God Said

We don't know exactly the content of Noah's message to his neighbors. He probably repeated often what the Lord had told him:

"Look! I am about to cover the earth with a flood that will destroy every living thing. Everything on earth will die!   Genesis 6:17

When we say what God says, we need not fear the outcome. God had assured Noah that he and his family would be saved (see Genesis 6:18). The righteous will always find grace in the eyes of the Lord.

The First Drops of Rain Made Everyone a Believer

When the ark was completed, Noah took his family inside, along with the animals God had instructed them to gather. Each day he continued to invite his neighbors and friends to join him in the ark, but they all declined his invitation.

Then, one day, when the first drop of rain fell from the sky, everyone suddenly became a believer, for now they realized that Noah had been right all along. In terror, the people ran to the ark and knocked on the door, but it was too late. God had shut the door (see Genesis 7:16).

Now everyone seemed to have faith. Now everyone was ready to repent of sin and accept God's forgiveness. This new-found faith, however, was false. As we have seen, faith is not believing what we see; it is believing what we don't see. Faith is not believing what we have; it's believing what we *"hope for."*

Imagine what went through Noah's mind as he heard his neighbors calling for him to open the door. "Noah," they called, "open the door! We believe. We're sorry for the way we treated you. Please open the door." He would have—if he could. But he couldn't. As always, God controlled the door to salvation.

Noah had to answer his neighbors, "I'm very sorry, but it's too late. God has shut the door, and I cannot open it."

> *The righteous will always find grace in the eyes of the Lord!*

As the storm raged and the flood waters rose, Noah and his family were safe inside the ark, while all around them the unbelieving world was turned into utter chaos. It could not have been easy for Noah to listen to the constant scorn of his neighbors. It could not have been easy for him to keep the spirits of his family high over such a long period of waiting. It could not have been easy to get all those animals together and get them into the ark. Yet he had fully obeyed, and now he and his loved ones were safe.

The story of Noah and the ark is one of the most popular Bible stories with people of all ages, but there is much more to remember about this great man. For instance, when Noah came out of the ark, the first thing he did was to erect an altar and worship God, using some of the animals that survived as sacrifices (see Genesis 8:20). God then entered into a covenant with him. The Noahic covenant was one of the major biblical covenants (see Genesis 9:9-10).

But Noah Was Not Superhuman

It would be easy to get the wrong idea about Abel and Enoch and Noah, and to conclude that they were somehow superhuman, different from the rest of us. Yes, they were *"righteous,"* they were *"just"* men, but they were not perfect.

In the case of Noah, the Scriptures even use the word *"perfect"* to describe him, but it soon becomes apparent to us that what God calls *"perfect"* is very different from what we call perfect and that man's perfection is susceptible to change. In later years, Noah planted a vineyard, drank the wine of his vineyard, and was found by his sons out wandering around naked. That he should be present in the gallery of faith should be encouraging to every single one of us. We, too, have our human weaknesses, but if we stay close to God, those human weaknesses will not prevent us from making Heaven our home or from having God's best for us in this life.

JESUS REMEMBERED NOAH

Jesus remembered Noah and spoke of the time of the end as being *as it was in the days of Noah"* (Luke 17:26, NKJ). This is an alarming comparison, for the ark did not save everyone. Only Noah and his wife and his sons and their wives entered the ark, and only those who entered were spared. These *"few"* righteous were saved, while the many ungodly perished (see 1 Peter 3:20). May God help us to heed the lessons learned through the faithful life of Noah.

If Noah could overcome in his time, you, too, can overcome the seemingly impossible situations life throws at you. Say it with me, and say it with faith: *"I Can Do This!"*

Now, go out and do it in Jesus' name.

CHAPTER 6

ABRAHAM: CONFIDENTLY LOOKING FOR A CITY

And even when he reached the land God promised him, he lived there by faith—for he was like a foreigner, living in a tent. And so did Isaac and Jacob, to whom God gave the same promise. Abraham did this because he was confidently looking forward to a city with eternal foundations, a city designed and built by God.

Hebrews 11:9-10

We return to Abraham because more is said of him in the Scriptures than of any other man, and that is as it should be. Abraham was, after all, as we have noted previously, *the father of [our] faith:*

The circumcision ceremony was a sign that Abraham

already had faith and that God had already accepted him and declared him to be righteous—even before he was circumcised. So Abraham is the spiritual father of those who have faith but have not been circumcised. They are made right with God by faith. And Abraham is also the spiritual father of those who have been circumcised, but only if they have the same kind of faith Abraham had before he was circumcised.

Romans 4:11-12

Aside from his faith in leaving Ur for Canaan to form a new nation, the faith of Abraham is demonstrated in Hebrews 11 in two other ways: in the way he lived in the land of Canaan and through his willingness to sacrifice his only son Isaac to God.

LIVING IN THE LAND

In the most literal sense, Abraham never did find the city he was looking for. God's promise to him was spiritual. He wanted to use Abraham to form a new and holy nation in order to bring forth His Word for all generations and in order to eventually bring the Savior into the world. The *"city whose builder and maker is God"* (KJV) was certainly not to be found in Canaan, yet when Abraham reached that land, he felt led to stop traveling and to settle down, sensing that this was indeed the land that God had promised him. It was, he knew, the place of his fulfillment.

In the years that followed, Abraham's faith would be

severely tested, for he must live as a foreigner in a strange land, dwelling among a strange people. This represented much hardship for him and also for his family. Foreigners, for example, were prohibited by law from owning property in Canaan, so Abraham, a man wonderfully blessed by God with this world's goods, would spend the rest of his life as a nomad, living in tents. He was an outsider, an intruder, a fact that must have produced powerful emotional trauma in him and in the other members of his extended family.

Yet, despite the fact that Abraham did not see this part of God's promise literally fulfilled, there is no record that he ever felt despair over it. He passed on the promise of God with confidence to Isaac and Jacob, *"heirs with him of the same promise"* (KJV). For this act, God remembered him and held him up as an example to all. Abraham showed us that the promises of God are worth waiting for.

In the years that followed, Abraham's faith would be severely tested, for he must live as a foreigner in a strange land, dwelling among a strange people!

THE SACRIFICE OF ISAAC

It was by faith that Abraham offered Isaac as a sacrifice when God was testing him. Abraham, who had received God's promises, was ready to sacrifice his only son, Isaac, though God had promised him, "Isaac is the son through whom your descendants will be counted." Abraham assumed that if Isaac died, God was able to bring him back to life again. And in a sense, Abraham did receive his son back from the dead.
Hebrews 11:17-19

The greatest trial of Abraham's faith came with the command to sacrifice Isaac, and this is one of the most misunderstood stories of the Old Testament. The sacrifice of Isaac is a case fairly unique in Bible history. The only comparable case involved a man known as Jephthah, and he, interestingly enough, is also among the heroes of faith lauded in the book of Hebrews (see Chapter 15).

Genesis gives this account of God's command to Abraham to sacrifice Isaac:

Later on God tested Abraham's faith and obedience.
"Abraham!" God called.
"Yes," he replied. "Here I am."
"Take your son, your only son—yes, Isaac, whom you love so much—and go to the land of Moriah. Sacrifice him there as a burnt offering on one of the mountains, which I will point out to you."   Genesis 22:1-2

Isaac was a miracle child, a child of promise and a child for whose birth Abraham and Sarah had waited many long years. They were sure he was God's blessing—for them and for all succeeding generations as well—and I doubt that any of us could imagine how much they really loved him. God understood Abraham's feelings for Isaac and called him *"your only son ... whom you love so much,"* but He still demanded the boy as a sacrifice.

Some would ask, "Why does God always want to take away the things we love most?" This story makes plain the fact that God does not want to do that. He only wants to test our love for Him. If we love someone or something more than we love God, even if it's someone or something that He has given to us, then He *should* take that person or that thing away from us—for our own spiritual good. If we love God above all else, we have nothing to fear from Him. He does not delight in taking things from His children. He delights in giving, in heaping upon us His greatest favors.

The fact is that God did *not* take Abraham's son. What He required of Abraham was only a test. But, oh, what a test!

This test did not indicate cruelty on God's part. It indicated His great love for Abraham. No person or thing must be allowed to stand between us and God, for He wants our undivided attention and our undiluted love.

The reason for Abraham's greatness can be seen in the next verse of Genesis:

The next morning Abraham got up early. He saddled his donkey and took two of his servants with him, along with his son Isaac. Then he chopped wood to build a fire for a burnt offering and set out for the place where God had told him to go. Genesis 22:3

Abraham was very human, and he must have been trying to reconcile in his own thinking everything that God had told him!

Nothing was said about an agonizing night of indecision on Abraham's part. Nothing was said about his questioning God, doubting God or accusing God. He got up early and set off to do what God had commanded him to do. Abraham obeyed—whether he liked it or not, whether he understood it or not and whether he agreed with it or not.

It took Abraham three days to reach the place of sacrifice, and those must have been three of the most difficult days of his life. For three long and agonizing days, his faith was tested, yet he didn't turn back, he didn't deviate from the proscribed path, and he didn't compromise his position. He went forward in obedience, doing everything that God required of him.

What was Abraham thinking about as he journeyed to the place of Isaac's imminent execution? We can only guess. He could not have fully understood that Isaac was a type of the coming Christ. He could not have fully understood why God was requiring *"the child of promise"* (Galatians 4:29). Still he didn't get angry with God, he didn't complain, he didn't protest, and he didn't refuse.

Abraham was very human, and he must have been trying to reconcile in his own thinking everything that God had told him. If Isaac was a child of promise and all future generations would be blessed through him, if Isaac was born by faith, by a miracle of God, and if God was now asking for him in sacrifice, that must mean only one thing: surely God would raise him up from the dead. And that became Abraham's security.

He knew that God was good, that God loved him, that God had promised him a great future, and that his future now depended upon Isaac, so there could be no other conclusion. God would raise Isaac from the dead. Abraham was sure of it.

These were Abraham's thoughts as he *"built an altar"* on Mt. Moriah. These were his thoughts as he *"laid the wood in order."* These were his thoughts as he *"bound Isaac his son, and laid him on the altar upon the wood."* And these were his thoughts as he *"stretched forth his hand, and took the knife to slay his son"* (KJV).

Abraham did everything God required of him. Then, as we all know, when God saw that Abraham was determined to obey Him, He intervened at the last moment and provided another sacrifice. He did not take Abraham's son.

The writer of Hebrews tells us that Abraham received

Isaac from the dead *"in a figure,"* because if Abraham had refused to give God his son, no doubt he would have lost him. It is only when we refuse to obey God that we end up as losers. We cannot lose when we willingly place ourselves on His team.

What God said to Abraham through the angel in that moment should inspire every one of us:

> *"Lay down the knife," the angel said. "Do not hurt the boy in any way, for now I know that you truly fear God. You have not withheld even your beloved son from me."*　　　　　　　Genesis 22:12

"Now I know." God has a right to test those who will be entrusted with His glory. When Abraham had proved his faith, God said, *"Now I know."* Then He gave Abraham an even greater promise:

> *"Because you have obeyed me and have not withheld even your beloved son, I swear by my own self that I will bless you richly. I will multiply your descendants into countless millions, like the stars of the sky and the sand on the seashore. They will conquer their enemies, and through your descendants, all the nations of the earth will be blessed—all because you have obeyed me."*　　　　　　　Genesis 22:16-18

Why was Abraham blessed above all men? God said, *"Because you have obeyed me and have not withheld even your beloved son,"* and again *"because you have obeyed me."*

These are God's reasons for a man's victory and prosperity—not a formula, not a memorized promise, not even faith in his own ability, but simple obedience brought about through His unerring faith in God Almighty.

When we prove faithful in the test of faith, God can then trust us with more, and it was at this moment that He confirmed His desire to give Abraham much more in life. God is ready to give each of us all that we can handle. If we can only pass today's tests, more blessings await us.

ABRAHAM'S FRAILTIES

Like Noah, Abraham was anything but a superman, and the Scriptures make no effort to hide his blemishes:

When there was a famine in the land, Abraham went to Egypt, a type of the world. God would later warn Isaac not to respond to famine in the way his father had.

On two occasions, Abraham required Sarah to lie and say that she was his sister, because he feared that foreign authorities would want her and would treat him badly as a result. Both times God saved him from his folly by a miracle.

When time passed and Sarah had not conceived, Abraham accepted her suggestion that he have a son by Hagar, her Egyptian maid. God was not pleased with that decision and did not bless *"the child of the bondwoman"* in the way he had promised to bless *"the child of the freewoman"* (Galatians 4:23, KJV).

No, Abraham was not superhuman. He was a man,

but he was a man of faith, and *"anything is possible to a person who believes."* They *"can do everything."*

God called Abraham His friend (see Isaiah 41:8), He was not ashamed to be called *"the God of Abraham"* (Matthew 22:32), Jesus called Paradise *"Abraham's bosom"* (Luke 16:22), He said that Abraham had foreseen His coming (see John 8:56), and Abraham is held up as an example in other New Testament passages (see Romans 4:1-3, Romans 4:18-25, Galatians 3:6-7, James 2:21 and 23). Is it any wonder that such a man is called the *"father of faith?"*

If Abraham could overcome in his day, then you, too, can face the seemingly impossible situations of your daily life and overcome. Say with me right now and say it with faith, *"I Can Do This!"*

Now, go out and do it in Jesus' name.

CHAPTER 7

SARAH: ABLE TO HAVE A CHILD

It was by faith that Sarah together with Abraham was able to have a child, even though they were too old and Sarah was barren. Abraham believed that God would keep his promise. And so a whole nation came from this one man, Abraham, who was too old to have any children—a nation with so many people that, like the stars of the sky and the sand on the seashore, there is no way to count them. Hebrews 11:11-12

Abraham could not produce a son by himself. Sarah also needed to act in faith. In the end, Abraham was able to produce descendents *"as the stars of the sky in multitude, and as the sand which is by the sea shore innumerable"* (KJV), but only because of the faith of Sarah.

The Curse of Barrenness

Sarah is described in scripture as being a very beautiful and desirable woman, but a woman whose happiness was incomplete because she was barren. That was a very serious matter in her day, and in many cultures, still today, barren women are looked down upon. In Sarah's time, barrenness was considered to be a curse, and the majority seemingly imagined that something must be wrong with any woman who was barren (perhaps she had committed some secret sin), and, therefore, barren women were held up to ridicule and scorn.

In many cultures, still today, barren women are looked down upon!

After living most of her adult life under this curse of barrenness, Sarah received a promise from God that she would indeed conceive and bear a son. We can only imagine her joy at that moment. That joy, however, turned to ashes when years passed and she still had not conceived. We can understand her impatience, because time seemed to be running out for her.

Enter Hagar

After living in Canaan for ten years, Sarah finally gave up hope of conceiving and convinced Abraham that they had misunderstood the promise of God and that he should, therefore, take Hagar, her Egyptian servant, as a concubine and have children by her. Abraham accepted this suggestion all too readily, and his precipitous action eventually caused a serious problem in the family.

Sarah underestimated what her own reaction would be to Abraham's willingness to take another woman, and she was further angered when Hagar quickly conceived. It was not long before Sarah despised her faithful servant and was determined to get her out of the house at any cost. When she treated Hagar harshly, the Egyptian woman fled, taking her son, Abraham's child, with her.

What a sad state of affairs! But God was not finished with Sarah and would, in time, bring to pass all of His promises for her life.

SARAH LAUGHED

The thing that is most remembered about Sarah is the fact that she laughed when she overheard the angels talking with her husband in the tent about the child she would bear. It is true that she laughed (see Genesis 18:12) and that she compounded her fault by then denying that she had laughed (see Genesis 18:13-15), but it should not surprise us that Sarah was not perfect. If the men in the list of heroes were imperfect, why should we expect the women to be any different? Sarah was human, and she was influenced by the circumstances of her life. She felt limited by time and by the natural forces of life. And which of us is different in this respect?

Sarah should not have doubted what she was hearing from the angel because God had already given her a new name that meant *"mother of princes"* or *"mother of nations"* (Genesis 17:15-16). Some have interpreted her laugh to mean that she was a strong-willed, doubting, disrespectful and impatient woman. But if that were true, why then would her name appear in this list of heroes?

Sarah's situation was so incredible that we cannot blame her for laughing. Consider the facts: Abraham was already seventy-five when he left Haran. After they reached the Promised Land, ten more years passed without them having children. That was the moment when she suggested that Abraham use Hagar as a surrogate mother. It was a wrong decision, and everyone suffered because of it, but nowhere does the Bible suggest that Sarah was anything but a respectful and cooperative wife. After all, she followed her husband across deserts and dangerous territory to some "promised land" neither one of them knew anything about.

The apostle Peter did not remember Sarah as being disrespectful:

Sarah obeyed her husband, Abraham, when she called him her master. You are her daughters when you do what is right without fear of what your husbands might do. 1 Peter 3:6

Yes, Sarah laughed, but Abraham laughed too. In fact, Abraham laughed before Sarah did:

Then Abraham fell upon his face, and laughed, and said in his heart, Shall a child be born unto him that is an hundred years old? and shall Sarah, that is ninety years old, bear?   Genesis 17:17, KJV

Can you picture it? Abraham, the prospective father, was already one hundred, and Sarah, the prospective mother, was already ninety. According to the Scriptures, they were both *"old and well stricken in age."* Sarah was certainly well past the childbearing age:

Now Abraham and Sarah were old and well stricken in age; and it ceased to be with Sarah after the manner of women.   Genesis 18:11, KJV

Paul later categorized the body of Abraham and the womb of Sarah as both being *"dead"* (Romans 4:19, KJV). Therefore, when we read the story of Sarah's laughter in context, it becomes easy to understand exactly why she laughed:

And since Abraham and Sarah were both very old, and Sarah was long past the age of having children, she laughed silently to herself. "How could a worn-out woman like me have a baby?" she thought. "And when my master—my husband—is also so old?"
                    Genesis 18:11-12

No wonder Sarah laughed! You would have laughed too.

All of us have moments of weakness and doubt. The promises of God are so incredible, meaning unbelievable. These promises sometimes seem to have no relationship to reality. As long as we insist on looking at our circumstances, we can only laugh. From the natural standpoint, there is no way that we can have what God has promised us.

When the Lord questioned Sarah's laugh, it suddenly dawned on her that laughing was inappropriate under the circumstances, that laughing was a sign of doubt and that her laughter in this situation was insulting to God. As she considered the seriousness of Who was speaking, she repented of her laughter, and she laughed no more ... until God gave her reason for a real laugh.

It happened the day Isaac was born, for on that day Sarah declared:

"God has brought me laughter! All who hear about this will laugh with me. For who would have dreamed that I would ever have a baby? Yet I have given Abraham a son in his old age!"   Genesis 21:6-7

What does this teach us? Those who deny their fallibility and insist on their perfection are doomed to failure, but those who recognize their human frailties and work to overcome them can be victorious. If we recognize doubt when it exists in us, confess it and ask the Lord to forgive us and strengthen us, there is no reason we cannot go forward in Him. He has not demanded that we be superhuman, only that we believe.

JOHN THE BAPTIST HAD HIS MOMENTS OF DOUBT

Even John the Baptist had his moments of doubt. During his time of imprisonment, he began to wonder if Jesus really was the Christ, and he sent men to his cousin to ask Him that very question. Jesus was compelled to send John this message in return:

The blind see, the lame walk, the lepers are cured, the deaf hear, the dead are raised to life, and the Good News is being preached to the poor.
Matthew 11:5

That answer satisfied John's doubt. When you find doubt in your heart, remember that Sarah eventually received her promises:

And the LORD visited Sarah AS HE HAD SAID, and the LORD did unto Sarah AS HE HAD SPOKEN.
Genesis 21:1, KJV

(Emphasis Added)

When the Lord questioned Sarah's laugh, it suddenly dawned on her that laughing was inappropriate under the circumstances!

God never fails to fulfill His promises—when we push aside our doubts and determine to trust Him.

87

Abraham sorely missed Sarah when she died (see Genesis 23:2). Her death ended a great chapter in the history of the fledgling nation of Israel. But because she was a woman of such great faith, she has caused all generations to laugh with her over the miracle God did in response to humility.

Considering the circumstances of her life, if Sarah could overcome, then you, too, can face the seemingly impossible situations of your daily life and overcome. Say with me right now, and say it with faith, *"I Can Do This!"*

Now, go out and do it in Jesus' name.

CHAPTER 8

ISAAC: BLESSING HIS SONS

It was by faith that Isaac blessed his two sons, Jacob and Esau. He had confidence in what God was going to do in the future.   Hebrews 11:20

As the miracle child of Abraham and Sarah, Isaac received the promise passed on to him by his parents. He had many good qualities and is described by the Bible as a humble man, a man of meditation and prayer, a loving man and a man of peace. In the Hebrews' record, however, the faith of Isaac was demonstrated in one simple act: he *"blessed Jacob and Esau concerning things to come"* (KJV). What this means is that Isaac accepted, by faith, the promise his father had entrusted to him and, by faith, passed it on to his two sons, Jacob and Esau.

Not Affected by the Generation Gap

Isaac was not affected by the generation gap. He did not automatically reject as "old-fashioned," "out-of-date," or "irrelevant-to-the-present-situation" everything that his parents had taught him—as many of a younger generation are tempted to do. He believed and accepted the promises of God as they had been given to his parents, and he passed them on in the same way to the next generation. That's faith.

Like his father before him, Isaac lived his entire life without seeing the physical fulfillment of the promise God had given them. Both Abraham and Isaac saw the fulfillment of many other promises from God, but the specific promises in question were for a future time and a future people. Still, like his father before him, Isaac did not stop believing and speaking to his sons *"concerning things to come."* The fact that these events had not happened in his lifetime did not discourage him and did not make him doubt the promises. "They will come to pass," he assured Jacob and Esau.

No Coattails in the Kingdom

Isaac did not ride into the Kingdom on the coattails of his father. As the popular saying goes, "God has no grandchildren," and each of us must develop his or her own personal relationship with the Creator. Isaac had to stand on his own faith in the goodness of God, and he also had to be tested—just as his father was tested before him.

ISAAC: BLESSING HIS SONS

When Isaac married Rebekah at the age of forty, he discovered that she was unable to conceive, as his mother had been unable to conceive. He had to intercede with God on his wife's behalf and, when he did, God did a miracle for them. The God of Abraham was proving that He could be the God of Isaac too.

Like his father, Isaac was tempted to go to Egypt in the time of famine (see Genesis 26:1-3). He was tempted to use his father's "she-is-my-sister trick" (see Genesis 26:7). He also had many of the same problems Abraham experienced with his neighbors (see Genesis 26:19-35). In the end, Isaac refused to strive for what was rightfully his. He knew that God would make room for him:

His shepherds also dug in the Gerar Valley and found a gushing spring. But then the local shepherds came and claimed the spring. "This is our water," they said, and they argued over it with Isaac's herdsmen. So Isaac named the well "Argument," because they had argued about it with him. Isaac's men then dug another well, but again

> *Like his father before him, Isaac lived his entire life without seeing the physical fulfillment of the promise God had given them!*

there was a fight over it. So Isaac named it "Opposition." Abandoning that one, he dug another well, and the local people finally left him alone. So Isaac called it "Room Enough," for he said, "At last the LORD has made room for us, and we will be able to thrive."

Genesis 26:19-22

Isaac Also Was Not Perfect

Like his father before him, Isaac was not perfect, but he knew Someone who was perfect, and his simple faith in God never wavered. He lived a wonderfully rich life, and when he died he was said to be *"full of days"* (Genesis 35:29, KJV). Like Abraham before him, he lived in the physical and financial prosperity of God (see Genesis 26:12-14). His Gentile neighbors took note of these blessings:

The Philistines became jealous of him. Genesis 26:14

Abimelech asked Isaac to leave the country. "Go somewhere else," he said, "for you have become too rich and powerful for us." Genesis 26:16

They replied, "We can plainly see that the LORD is with you." Genesis 26:28

We sent you away from us in peace. And now look how the Lord has blessed you! Genesis 26:29

THE GOD OF ISAAC

As with Abraham, God was not ashamed to be called *"the God of Isaac"* (Genesis 28:13 and Matthew 22:32). These are the rewards of simple faith.

If Isaac could face the giants of his day and overcome, then you, too, can face the seemingly impossible situations of your daily life and overcome. Say with me, and say it with faith, *"I Can Do This!"*

Now, go out and do it in Jesus' name.

CHAPTER 9

JACOB: BOWING IN WORSHIP

It was by faith that Jacob, when he was old and dying, blessed each of Joseph's sons and bowed in worship as he leaned on his staff.   Hebrews 11:21

The appearance of Jacob in the list of the heroes of faith should serve as an encouragement to millions of believers, for his life was a series of ups and downs, successes and failures, victories and defeats. God knew the final outcome before his birth and declared that, of the twins, *"the elder"* would *"serve the younger"* (Genesis 25:23, KJV). God was not taking sides. He just knew what kind of decisions Esau would make in life and what kind of decisions Jacob would make. It was Jacob who, by his decision to follow the faith of his fathers, was responsible for moving the balance of God's favor to his side.

Faith Did Not Come Easily to Jacob

Faith did not come easily to Jacob, however. Because he wrestled with his brother in birth, his name meant *"supplanter"* or *"deceiver"* (Genesis 25:26, KJV). Names meant a lot in those days, and perhaps Jacob was destined (in the flesh) to be a deceiver, but God had better things in mind for him.

> *There was certainly nothing good about the way Jacob deceived his father to gain material blessing, and nothing good came of it!*

There was certainly nothing good about the way Jacob deceived his father to gain material blessing, and nothing good came of it. He received absolutely nothing as a result of his duplicity. In fact, his deceit forced him to flee from home and from everything he held dear.

His mother had suggested the plot to deceive Isaac, because she favored Jacob over Esau. She did not foresee that her suggestion would separate her most beloved son from her for many years to come. She imagined that he could come home in just a few days.

Part of God's Plan for His Life

But Jacob's journey was part of God's plan for his life, and it was on this journey that he had an encounter with God at Bethel and made a vow to live for His Maker and to do His will. His vow was this:

"If God will be with me and protect me on this journey and give me food and clothing, and if he will bring me back safely to my father, then I will make the Lord my God. This memorial pillar will become a place for worshiping God, and I will give God a tenth of everything he gives me."
Genesis 28:20-22

Jacob's life away from home was not a happy one. His father-in-law deceived him on his wedding night, giving him the older sister, Leah, instead of the woman he loved. This double-dealing was particularly troubling, seeing that Jacob had already worked seven years for the right to wed Rachel.

When Laban saw that Jacob was still love-sick for Rachel, he required another seven years of work for her hand. But even after Jacob had worked out his fourteen years, Laban continued to take unfair advantage of him. Only a miracle from God saved Jacob from walking away from the whole situation empty-handed (see Genesis 31:7-9).

Years of Infighting

After Jacob insisted on marrying the woman he loved, despite the fact that he was already joined to her sister, many years of bitter infighting developed between the sisters. This infighting saddened Jacob and poisoned his children.

The sons of Laban, who thus became the brothers-in-law of Jacob, also hated, mistrusted, and mistreated him (see Genesis 31:1). Eventually, God called Jacob to return to his own land and leave his in-laws behind (see Genesis 31:3 and Genesis 31:11-13).

Leaving the land of their father must have been difficult for the daughters of Laban and perhaps even for Jacob, considering his new-found prosperity. Change is not a pleasant thing for most of us. But Jacob believed what God had told him. He would be blessed in the land of promise and, indeed, he had stayed away too long already. The attitude of Laban just helped him on his way, and sometimes we need this type of encouragement. God takes the comfort out of our nests so that we will move on to the better things He has awaiting us. It was time for Jacob to test his wings.

THE JOURNEY BACK HOME

No sooner had Jacob begun his journey home than he encountered some angels (see Genesis 32:1-2). This made him know that God was surely with him and would prosper his way. The next day he sent messengers to tell Esau that he was coming home and, with them, he sent word that he had a vast number of animals and servants for Esau as a peace offering.

When those messengers returned, saying that Esau

was coming to meet him with *"four hundred men,"* Jacob *"was greatly afraid and distressed"* (Genesis 32:7, KJV). Deceit pays such great dividends that Jacob was still collecting years later and couldn't be sure what Esau's present intentions were. The prospect of having his family and all that he had worked for through the years of his absence destroyed in a single battle terrified him. Faith destroys fear, but sin begets it.

There was one positive aspect of Jacob's fear. At least it all caused him to pray (see Genesis 32:9-12).

HAVING TO FACE ESAU

Jacob prepared the gifts he had designated for his brother and sent them ahead. That night he was alone and got serious with God, wrestling with the Lord until dawn and insisting on being blessed before he would let go. It was that night in which he lost the designation Jacob, *"deceiver,"* and instead became Israel, *"Prince with God"* (Genesis 32:28).

The meeting with Esau turned out to be a happy one. His brother had forgiven him for his deceit and received him with joy. Esau had also prospered and didn't need Jacob's gifts, but Jacob insisted on giving them anyway. How good God is!

MORE HEARTACHE

Not everything went this well for Jacob. A little further along the way home, his daughter Dinah was defiled by a local prince. When the sons of Jacob took vengeance upon the offending tribe, their conduct left a bad testimony in the land. Jacob complained to his sons, imagining that he would now be attacked by these people (see Genesis 34:30). God told Jacob that if he would return to Bethel and renew his vows, he would have nothing to fear. He obeyed, but first he demanded of his family members and servants that they give up any false gods they were carrying and that they purify themselves in preparation for meeting God.

Jacob had reason to be concerned, for false gods were indeed found in the camp, and they were destroyed. The result of this cleansing was notable:

> *When they set out again, terror from God came over the people in all the towns of that area, and no one attacked them.* Genesis 35:5

After another remarkable encounter with God at Bethel, Jacob went on his way. Not surprisingly, life did not suddenly become a bed of roses for him. Rachel, his beloved, died giving birth to Benjamin on the way back home (see Genesis 35:16-20). After they were in the land, terrible jealousies arose between Jacob's sons, resulting in Joseph's being sold into slavery, an act that threatened to bring Jacob's soul down to the grave, since Joseph was his favorite of all the sons (see Genesis 37:35). This great sorrow would later be turned into rejoicing, as God exalted Joseph in

Egypt and used him to preserve the fledgling nation of Israel. This became necessary because many of Jacob's sons had taken heathen wives and were slowly turning away from God and toward paganism.

Jacob's eldest son Judah and his two sons displeased the Lord so much that the sons were slain (see Genesis 38). Jacob suffered many such ups and downs in his life, but one thing remained constant throughout. God loved him with a special love. He said:

> *"I have loved you," says the Lord.*
> *"Yet you say, 'In what way have You loved us?'*
> *Was not Esau Jacob's brother?"*
> *Says the Lord.*
> *"Yet Jacob I have loved;*
> *But Esau I have hated,*
> *And laid waste his mountains and his heritage*
> *For the jackals of the wilderness."*
>
> Malachi 1:2-3, NKJ

> *God told Jacob that if he would return to Bethel and renew his vows, he would have nothing to fear!*

As it is written, "Jacob I have loved, but Esau I have hated." Romans 9:13, NKJ

Jacob's Last Act

Before he died, Jacob entrusted to his children and grandchildren all the promises of God that remained unfulfilled in his lifetime. Despite every struggle and all that life had thrown at him, he was still ready to worship his Creator. His strength was ebbing, and he was forced to lean on his staff for support, but he called all his family together, passed on the promises of God to his spiritual heir, Joseph, and to Joseph's two sons, Manasseh and Ephraim, and prophesied to all the others (see Genesis 49:1). Jacob may have felt rather weak physically, but his faith was as strong as ever. His eyesight may have been failing, but his faith in God was not.

He told each of his children what he knew God's will to be for them in the future, and then he charged them not to bury him in Egypt, but in the crypt of his grandfather Abraham. He was grateful for what Joseph had done for them in Egypt, but he was not about to forget the land of promise, the land of blessing. That's where he belonged.

When Jacob had finished everything he wanted to say to his children and grandchildren, he died (see Genesis 49:33).

The Most Beautiful Commentary

The most beautiful commentary on Jacob's death was given by the writer of Hebrews:

By faith Jacob, when he was a-dying, blessed both the sons of Joseph; and worshipped, leaning upon the top of his staff.   Hebrews 11:21, KJV

Jacob had lived by faith, and he was now ready to die by faith. As he drew his final breath, he was still praising God. Nothing had changed. God would not fail. He was sure of it. Abraham, then Isaac, and then Jacob ... three generations had successfully carried forward their simple faith in God. How wonderful!

If Jacob could overcome in the difficult circumstances of his life, then you, too, can face the seemingly impossible situations of your daily life and overcome. Say with me, and say it with faith, *"I Can Do This!"*

Now, go out and do it in Jesus' name.

CHAPTER 10

JOSEPH: BEING SO SURE OF IT

And it was by faith that Joseph, when he was about to die, confidently spoke of God's bringing the people of Israel out of Egypt. He was so sure of it that he commanded them to carry his bones with them when they left!   Hebrews 11:22

The Genesis account relates that Joseph was the favorite son of Jacob *"because he was the son of his old age"* (Genesis 37:3, KJV), but there was a much deeper reason. Most of Jacob's sons were spoiled by the constant bickering of their mothers and eventually intermarried with pagan wives, bringing grief to their father and shame to the entire clan by abandoning the God of Israel. Joseph was not only a spiritual child, he proved to be the salvation of the entire family and, indeed, of the entire nation.

Joseph Was a Child of Dreams

When Joseph began receiving dreams from God at a very early age, his brothers hated him for it. Not only did they not receive the message of the dreams, but they rejected him as a person and resented him for having such dreams.

It may well be that Joseph used poor judgement in telling his brothers about his dreams. Lack of wisdom would not be unusual for a boy of his age. Perhaps he should have sensed that his brothers would not rejoice with him and that they would, instead, be repelled by what he said.

Perhaps Jacob also used poor judgement in showing favor openly to Joseph. Many parents make that same mistake. Whatever the case, any lack of wisdom on the part of Jacob or Joseph could not excuse the actions of the other brothers. They were not moved by any lack of wisdom on Jacob's part or on Joseph's part, but by *"envy"*:

And the patriarchs, moved with envy, sold Joseph into Egypt.   Acts 7:9, KJV

There is no excuse for hating those who hear from God, when we should be hearing from Him ourselves. There is no excuse for hating someone for doing what we should be doing. It is a fact, however, that God's blessings engender misunderstanding and resentment in those who reject them.

Whatever the reason, Joseph was mistreated by his

brothers as a result of his dreaming. One day, when they caught him alone in the field far from home, they decided to get rid of him once and for all. The first thing they did was to strip him of his many-colored coat, the symbol of his father's love. Then they put him into a deep pit and left him there.

JOSEPH IN THE PIT

What was Joseph thinking as he awaited his fate in that terrible pit? Years later, he would reveal to his brothers that it had all been for *"good," "to save much people"*:

> *But as for you, ye thought evil against me; but God meant it unto good, to bring to pass, as it is this day, to save much people alive.*
> Genesis 50:20, KJV

There is no excuse for hating those who hear from God, when we should be hearing from Him ourselves!

But how long did it take Joseph to realize that what his brothers had done to him, intending to harm him, would actually serve the will of God for all of them? We often don't understand what God is doing in us at the moment and must accept His will by faith. We can do that because we know that He is good, that He loves us and that He has promised to work for our benefit always.

"If God is good, then why am I in this pit?" some might think. "If God is good, then why do my brothers hate me and pick on me so terribly?" Joseph's dream showed that his brothers would one day bow before him, but right now they were not bowing.

Many jumbled thoughts must have gone through Joseph's mind in that pit. Did God know where he was at that moment? Did God understand what the other sons of Jacob were doing to him? Did God care? Did God even hear Joseph's cry for help?

It is how we react to life's pits that makes us or breaks us. We are not defined by the good times we encounter but by the adversity we face and conquer. Nothing is said in the Bible about Joseph's thoughts in that moment, for nothing needed to be said. He was a man of faith. He believed God, and God was in control—despite all the appearances to the contrary.

SOLD INTO SLAVERY

When the brothers saw a caravan approaching, Judah got an idea. If they could sell Joseph to the caravan owners, they could rid themselves of the pesky fellow and make a little money on the side. Just that easily and quickly, it was done. Joseph was bound and led away, and his brothers went home twenty pieces of silver richer then they had been that morning.

Joseph was seventeen years old and had never been

JOSEPH: BEING SO SURE OF IT

separated from his father. Some never recover from such unfairness in life, but Joseph was destined to greatness, and he knew it. No caravan could keep him from it. No jealous brother could prevent his ascendancy. They were not hurting him; they were helping him to achieve God's will for his life. God had to get him down to Egypt because he was going to rule under the Pharaoh. These angry brothers and these greedy traders were just providing Joseph with a free ride to his destiny. And he didn't even have a passport.

Some would have considered those to be the darkest moments of their lives, but to Joseph, that caravan represented his ride to destiny. What an exciting opportunity!

There are always two ways to look at things, and the choice is ours. Problem or opportunity! Tragedy or triumph! You choose. The result is according to your faith. Win or lose, the choice is yours.

Joseph's brothers smeared the blood of a slain animal over the many-colored coat and sent it back to Jacob, saying that some wild beast had killed the boy. Jacob sorely grieved the loss of his most-beloved son, but Joseph was on his way to Egypt.

How was Joseph treated along the way? What was his reaction to being bound, to being forced to obey every whim of his captors, to being treated as so much meat for the marketplace? Nothing is said at all in the biblical narrative about this phase of Joseph's life. And that's because it didn't matter. This was only a stepping-stone to greater glory and honor. Joseph must endure what he must endure, for he was destined to reign.

Servitude in Egypt

One short verse gives us the capsule of Joseph's transition from captivity in the caravan to servitude in Egypt:

> *And the Midianites sold him into Egypt unto Potiphar, an officer of Pharaoh's, and captain of the guard.*
> Genesis 37:36, KJV

For the moment, Joseph is left in servitude, while life in Canaan goes on!

Nothing more is said. That was that, and at this point, the Genesis narrative turns back to the other brothers and their life in Canaan. For the moment, Joseph is left in servitude, while life in Canaan goes on. Young people married, babies were born, and the sick and elderly passed on to their reward. It must have seemed, at times, to Joseph's brothers, almost as if he had never existed. No doubt they all tried to push the memory of him from their minds and get on with their lives. Joseph, however, was not totally forgotten. What God did for him in Egypt is one of the most amazing stories in the Bible:

> *The LORD was with Joseph and blessed him greatly as he served in the home of his Egyptian master.*

Potiphar noticed this and realized that the LORD *was with Joseph, giving him success in everything he did. So Joseph naturally became quite a favorite with him. Potiphar soon put Joseph in charge of his entire household and entrusted him with all his business dealings. From the day Joseph was put in charge, the* LORD *began to bless Potiphar for Joseph's sake. All his household affairs began to run smoothly, and his crops and livestock flourished. So Potiphar gave Joseph complete administrative responsibility over everything he owned. With Joseph there, he didn't have a worry in the world, except to decide what he wanted to eat!*

Genesis 39:2-6

God had a purpose for everything that happened to Joseph, and Joseph, rather than cursing God, rather than becoming bitter with his circumstances, rather than using his mistreatment as an excuse to do evil himself, did his best in every situation in which he found himself. That's faith, and God honored him for it and gradually exalted him.

How much time had gone by since Joseph arrived in Egypt? We cannot say for sure. How long did it take for Joseph to gain the respect and trust of his owner? We don't know exactly. The important thing is that he did the right thing—whatever period of time was involved.

SUCCESS BRINGS TRIALS OF ITS OWN

Very soon Joseph was to learn that success brings trials of its own. They may be new and very different trials, but that doesn't make them any easier. Authority is a wonderful thing, but it exposes you to the "groupie" mentality of those who have nothing better to do in life than entertain themselves with the plaything of the moment. Before long, Joseph was the object of attention of Potiphar's wife. She wanted him and was determined to have him at any cost (see Genesis 39:7-12).

Her teasing went on over a period of time, until it became constant. She did it *"day by day"* (KJV). We can only guess at her motivation. Perhaps her husband had little time for her, or perhaps he was unfaithful to her. Perhaps, in her own mind, she was justified in making advances to Joseph, or perhaps she didn't need any justification. Those who are dedicated to self-gratification rarely weigh the consequences of their acts or care who they might hurt in the process. They only live for the moment. This woman was bold about it.

This placed Joseph in an extremely difficult position. The woman, by virtue of being the wife of Potiphar, was his owner, and he was required to obey her, to wait hand and foot on her and to do her bidding—whatever it happened to be at the moment. What could he do?

There is nothing to indicate that Potiphar's wife was not a very attractive and desirable woman, and Joseph was far from home and family, lonely,and in a strange land among a strange people. Who would have blamed him if he had succumbed to her constant urgings and sought comfort in her arms? After all, she commanded him to do it. And if he did not obey, what might she do? The wrath of a scorned woman is legendary.

What kept Joseph from falling into the trap set for him by this beguiling woman? Did he somehow understand that doing what she wanted would cause him to lose his place in the history of Israel and become like other men? The Scriptures record only that he was determined not to sin against God (see Genesis 39:9). Joseph remained loyal to God, loyal to his master and loyal to his commitments.

Joseph might well have been able to sin with Ms. Potiphar without her husband ever learning the truth of what had happened, but he would not have been able to live with himself if he had failed in this way. It didn't matter that perhaps Potiphar didn't deserve such a fine woman (if she was, indeed, a fine woman). It didn't matter that God had seemed to forget Joseph and had left him in bondage in a strange land. He was sure that God had not forgotten him and that he was in that place for a purpose, a purpose that he must keep uppermost in his thinking.

If Joseph had forgotten his purpose, sinning might have come to him more easily, but he couldn't forget. He knew that his dreams were from God and that God would bring them to pass—somehow and in some way. He made the decision to get out of Potiphar's house as fast as he could, leaving his cloak in the hands of the woman clutching at him.

THE REACTION OF A WOMAN SCORNED

Ms. Potiphar reacted exactly as we might imagine. She screamed in rage, calling for help and suggesting that

113

Joseph had attacked her, and she held up the proof—the garment he had left in her hands. She told her husband the same lie (see Genesis 39:16-18), and she used prejudice *("the Hebrew")* and Potiphar's manly pride as tools to incite him against Joseph.

Perhaps she had warned Joseph that she would do this very thing if he did not willingly submit to her wishes. After all, who would know? Who would care? And if Joseph refused to cooperate, this would be her revenge. In the end, however, he would not yield, and now she felt she must destroy him.

Potiphar was understandably enraged and had Joseph thrown into prison. It is so easy for the ungodly to believe an accusation against the righteous. "I knew there was something strange about that person," they say. "They just seemed too good to be true."

AWAKENING BEHIND BARS

The next morning, when Joseph awoke, he was not in his room in the slave quarters of Potiphar's house, where he had awakened every morning now for some time. When his eyes opened, the first thing he noticed was the closeness of the walls, the thickness of the bars, and the sturdiness of the door. Then the reality came flooding back. He was in Pharaoh's infamous prison house.

Being punished for something we have done wrong is one thing. It's never easy to bear, but at least we know we deserve it. But being punished for something we didn't do is always much harder to bear. In actuality, Joseph was being punished for faithfulness, for loyalty, for having done the right thing. Jesus called it being *"persecuted for righteousness sake"* (KJV). He said:

> *God blesses you when you are mocked and persecuted and lied about because you are my followers. Be happy about it! Be very glad! For a great reward awaits you in heaven. And remember, the ancient prophets were persecuted, too.*
>
> Matthew 5:11-12

It's a blessing to be wrongfully accused and wrongfully treated—when it comes as a result of our having done the right thing. It may not seem to be a blessing at the moment, and I can imagine that Joseph must have wondered, over and over again, if he had done the right thing. In his heart, however, he knew that he had made a right decision, and he determined to make the best of his situation. This was just another pit. He had gotten out of the first one, and he would get out of this one too. God had a great future planned for him, and no prison could keep him from it. He was sure of that.

Perhaps she had warned Joseph that she would do this very thing if he did not willingly submit to her wishes!

Just as Joseph had prospered in Potiphar's house, he now prospered in Pharaoh's prison:

*But the L*ORD *was with Joseph there, too, and he granted Joseph favor with the chief jailer. Before long, the jailer put Joseph in charge of all the other prisoners and over everything that happened in the prison. The chief jailer had no more worries after that, because Joseph took care of everything. The L*ORD *was with him, making everything run smoothly and successfully.*

Genesis 39:21-23

Many people curse God in their prison and are dragged down into despair and self-pity, but Joseph prospered, and you can too. When we face life's pits and prisons, we must know that we may be facing the final test that will prepare us to be the prime ministers of tomorrow.

This is always the purpose of our tests. A loving God never intends for the difficult tests He sends our way to damage our souls. He is testing our resolve and trying our faith to prepare us for greatness.

God was ready to do something decisive in Egypt. He was ready to save the nation of Israel. He was ready, but was Joseph ready? His final test was about to come, and it would prove whether or not the lad was ready to rule.

Always remember: the greater the test you must face, the greater the victory that awaits you. Be faithful, and you will emerge from the dungeon to rule and reign.

ATTUNED TO GOD

It was in this prison, through constant communion with God, that Joseph became an interpreter of hard dreams. It was his deepening relationship with God (perhaps forged out of sheer desperation, loneliness, and the attempt to understand his circumstances) that enabled Joseph to have an answer for the king's servants who dreamed and, later, for the dreams of the Pharaoh himself.

This is not to say that Joseph enjoyed prison life. He most certainly did not. When he interpreted the butler's dream and told him that he would be restored to Pharaoh's favor, he added:

> *Please have some pity on me when you are back in his [Pharaoh's] favor. Mention me to Pharaoh, and ask him to let me out of here. For I was kidnapped from my homeland, the land of the Hebrews, and now I'm here in jail, but I did nothing to deserve it.*
>
> Genesis 40:14-15

Joseph believed that God would get him out of prison, and he was hoping that this butler might be the vessel God used. But he was to be disappointed again, for this man, whom he had helped so dramatically, forgot him (see Genesis 40:23). It happens, and it happens often.

But don't worry when people forget you. Don't worry when someone who has promised to remember

117

your need doesn't remember. Don't worry! There is Someone who has not forgotten you. There is a reason for you being in the dungeon, and God will soon bring you forth to serve. Just trust Him!

Two More Years Passed

> *Don't worry when someone who has promised to remember your need doesn't remember!*

Two more years passed before Pharaoh had his fateful dream, two years in which the prison food did not improve, and the dingy walls did not become cheery. Two whole years! That must have seemed like a lifetime to Joseph, as it would to any one of us.

During this time, Joseph had a choice. He could become bitter (because he was losing the best years of his youth locked up and forgotten in some dingy prison and because everyone was mistreating him, lying about him, and forgetting their vows to help him), or he could think of two whole years as a wonderful opportunity to prepare himself for what lay ahead. This latter is exactly what Joseph chose to do.

When Pharaoh had his dream, Joseph was not sulking in the depths of the prison, planning his revenge against those who had wronged him when he finally did get out of that awful place. He was talking to God about his future and preparing himself for it. When the dream was dreamed, he was ready to reveal the interpretation.

PHARAOH'S DREAM

The story of the fat years and the lean years and the young man who was appointed by the Pharaoh to store up food in Egypt during the fat years for use in the lean ones is one of the first stories we learn as children and one that continues to inspire us as adults. Despite the fact that he was still a young man, far from home and family, and that he had been wrongly imprisoned for several years, Joseph could still forget about his own problems long enough to concentrate on helping others. This was his destiny, not to complain about how cold the prison was or how many people had wronged him and how. He was not born to complain, but to reign.

When Joseph interpreted the king's dream and told him frankly what he considered to be the solution, Pharaoh was duly impressed. In a few short sentences, Joseph had spelled out, not only the problem, but also the solution that would save the entire nation and many surrounding nations as well. As Pharaoh thought of the need for a man he could place over this work, to carry out honestly and fairly the purchase and storage of grain against the lean years, he realized that he knew no one with as much wisdom as Joseph had just displayed. Indeed, the *"wise men"* of Egypt had failed to interpret the dream, let alone find a solution to the coming crisis. Joseph was his man:

Turning to Joseph, Pharaoh said, "Since God has revealed the meaning of the dreams to you, you are the wisest man in the land! I hereby appoint you to direct this project. You will manage my household and organize all my people. Only I will have a rank higher than yours. ... I hereby put you in charge of the entire land of Egypt." Genesis 41:39-41

That day Pharaoh took a special ring from his own hand and placed it on the finger of Joseph; he ordered a special garment to be placed on the youth and a gold chain to be hung around his neck. He placed Joseph in the next chariot behind his own, effectively making him second in command in the nation. And he also set about to find Joseph a suitable wife.

That morning Joseph had awakened as before to the reality of the dungeon, but he sensed that this was to be a new day. The next thing he knew he was riding behind Pharaoh and someone was crying out, "Bow the knee," and the Egyptian people were looking to him to save their nation.

The day all this happened, the Scriptures say, Joseph was *"thirty years old"* (Genesis 41:46). He had been seventeen when his brothers sold him into slavery, so between his period of service to Potiphar and his sojourn in the Egyptian prison, he had spent thirteen long years of his life. The experience of those thirteen years, however, had not destroyed Joseph, but rather had prepared him to serve in a greater capacity:

And people from surrounding lands also came to Egypt to buy grain from Joseph because the famine was severe throughout the world. Genesis 41:57

Suddenly the pit made sense. Suddenly the terrors of being taken from home and family and sold into slavery in a strange land made sense. Suddenly the treachery of Potiphar's wife made sense. Suddenly the years of imprisonment made sense. Thank God for his brothers. Thank God for Ms. Potiphar. Thank God for the forgetful butler. God had a purpose in everything that had befallen Joseph's life until this moment.

Joseph had known since he was very young that he would some day rule over others, but he had not imagined that it would come about in the way it did. He had clung to his faith in the pit and in the dungeon, and now he was ready to serve God in strength.

JOSEPH'S VERY HUMAN REACTION

When his first son was born, Joseph called him Manasseh because, he said, *"God has made me forget all my troubles and the family of my father"* (Genesis 41:51). He was very human and had suffered psychologically from the abusive way others had treated him, but God had made him forget.

Joseph called his second son Ephraim, saying: *"God has made me fruitful in this land of my suffering"* (Genesis 41:52). It was a most human reaction.

Then, one day, when his brothers came to Egypt,

seeking to buy grain, we see Joseph's struggle to relate to them, to forgive them for what they had done to him and to be reunited with them. In the end, Joseph not only forgave his brothers; he secured land for them and sustained them in the time of difficulty—all of them, together with their extended families (see Genesis 47:12).

The treachery of his brothers now made perfect sense. They intended it for harm, but God intended it for good. How could he not forgive them? It is a small person who cannot forgive the wrongs others have committed against him.

It was in this way that Jacob and all his sons and their families traveled to Egypt and lived in the land of Goshen. And the Hebrew people were preserved as a nation—because of a man of faith.

JOSEPH'S GREATEST ACT OF FAITH

In the Hebrew's gallery of heroes, Joseph is remembered for one great act of faith. Despite his position of prominence and authority in Egypt, despite the powerful influence he and his family had been able to exert over the Pharaoh, and despite their prosperity in the land of Goshen, Joseph recognized that their sojourn in Egypt was a temporary one and that the nation of Israel would one day be called to return to the land of promise. "When you go," he told his children, "don't leave my bones here. Take me with you":

"Soon I will die," Joseph told his brothers, "but God will

surely come for you, to lead you out of this land of Egypt. He will bring you back to the land he vowed to give to the descendants of Abraham, Isaac, and Jacob." Then Joseph made the sons of Israel swear an oath, and he said, "When God comes to lead us back to Canaan, you must take my body back with you." So Joseph died at the age of 110. They embalmed him, and his body was placed in a coffin in Egypt.
Genesis 50:24-26

In the end, Joseph not only forgave his brothers; he secured land for them and sustained them in the time of difficulty!

Some four hundred years later, Moses would carry out Joseph's request, taking the bones of the man of faith with him, as he led the Israelites back toward the Promised Land.

If Joseph could endure all that he did and still overcome, then you, too, can face the seemingly impossible situations of your daily life and overcome. Say with me and say it with faith, *"I Can Do This!"*

Now, go out and do it in Jesus' name.

CHAPTER 11

AMRAM AND JOCHEBED: HIDING A PROMISING SON

It was by faith that Moses' parents hid him for three months. They saw that God had given them an unusual child, and they were not afraid of what the king might do. Hebrews 11:23

The King James Version of the Bible begins this verse, with the words, *"By faith Moses,"* but it was the parents, not the child, who exercised faith in this case. An infant is trusting and open and learning, but an infant knows nothing yet of God and, therefore, cannot have faith in Him. It was the faith of Moses' parents (Amram, identified as a Levite, and his wife Jochebed) who caused Moses to be hidden so that his life could be spared. Moses could not have led the children out of Egypt if his parents had not risked their lives to protect him during his infancy.

AMRAM AND JOCHEBED?

> *We've all heard of Abraham, Isaac, and Jacob, Moses, Elijah, and David, but Amram and Jochebed?*

Mentioning Amram and Jochebed in the list of heroes of faith is the writer's way of honoring all such unsung heroes. We've all heard of Abraham, Isaac, and Jacob, Moses, Elijah, and David, but Amram and Jochebed? There are many such heroes of faith who never receive their just recognition in this life. Knowing, however, that God is a just God, we expect them to be exalted in His presence in due time.

Of Amram and Jochebed, we know only what we read here in Hebrews and the confirmation of these truths in the story of Exodus 2:1-10, the age-old story of Moses in the bulrushes. Jochebed gave birth to her son and successfully hid him from the Egyptians for three months. That, in itself, was an amazing feat of daring, considering the circumstances.

MOSES IN THE BULRUSHES

Most of us know the story well. When a new Pharaoh

came to power (a man who had never heard of Joseph and the blessing he and his people had been to Egypt), he became alarmed when he saw the prosperity of the Hebrews. If they were not somehow stopped, he decided, they would eventually overpower the Egyptians and take control of the Empire. Because of this, he forced the Hebrews into heavy bondage, and when they still prospered, he ordered all their newborn male babies to be slaughtered. It was Satan's attempt to destroy the coming deliverer, a startling resemblance to Herod's order to kill all boy babies in the time of Jesus.

Most Hebrew parents felt that they had no choice in this matter. They were slaves, after all. They must obey—or else. Amram and Jochebed, however, decided to defy the Pharaoh and to preserve Moses' life. That was an extraordinary decision on their part.

WHY DID THEY DO IT?

Why would these two people dare to do such a thing? Life was already extremely difficult for them, and it was getting more difficult every day. Why add to their problems by willfully disobeying the Pharaoh's command? What would motivate them to do such a rash thing? Hebrews gives two simple answers to these questions:

1. *They saw that God had given them an unusual child,* and
2. *They were not afraid of what the king might do.*

These are both amazing statements of faith. First, Amram and Jochebed saw something very special in their child. What could it have been? Was he bigger or stronger or brighter-eyed or more full of laughter than other children of a similar age? While there are differences in infants, these differences are not great enough for any expert to be able to predict what a given child might or might not do later in life. In the first three months of his life, Moses could not have done anything or said anything that would have convinced his parents that he was worth risking their lives for. And the fact that the other Hebrew families found no means of saving their beloved children shows what an unusual case this was. All of them loved their children, but one family found a way to preserve the life of their son.

The mysterious something that Amram and Jochebed saw in their child had to be spiritually discerned. It had to be felt, for it could not have been seen with the naked eye. It must have been perceived in the Spirit. This was a spiritual family, a family of faith, and God was showing them that He would soon deliver the Israelites from bondage and that their son had some important role to play in that deliverance.

Just how many details Amram and Jochebed knew we cannot be sure, but it doesn't matter. Faith doesn't require details. They somehow perceived the greatness of Moses' future, and that perception made them willing to risk their own lives to save his.

THEY WERE NOT AFRAID
OF THE KING'S COMMANDMENT

How could it be possible that humble slaves were not afraid of the Pharaoh of Egypt, the greatest, most powerful, and richest king in all the world at the time? The Pharaoh was the ruler of the Egyptian Empire. How could common men not fear him? It would be only natural for them to fear such a powerful man, especially since they themselves were mere slaves and so powerless.

The secret of the faith of Amram and Jochebed was that they feared the Invisible and Eternal King more than they feared the visible Pharaoh. Since they walked close to God, and since God showed them that His favor was upon Moses, they were not afraid to disobey the king's command. Instead, they were afraid not to obey God. Obeying God is never a risk, but disobeying always is.

AMRAM AND JOCHEBED PASSED
THEIR FAITH ON TO MOSES

The faith of Amram and Jochebed was passed on to Moses:

By faith he forsook Egypt, not fearing the wrath of the king: for he endured, as seeing him who is invisible.
Hebrews 11:27, KJV

Moses was blessed with parents of faith, and he owed them his very life. Not only did his parents keep his birth

129

secret, and not only did they hide him successfully for three months, but they received a cunning plan from God for his future. It was a plan that allowed Jochebed to raise Moses in his formative years and to impart to him, through the kind of teaching that only a mother can give, her faith in God. Faith is passed from mother and father to son and daughter, not as a genetic inheritance, but as a matter of teaching and practice. No doubt Amram and Jochebed had died by the time Moses finally led the people of Israel across the Red Sea into the wilderness and on their way home, but this couple was directly responsible for the great deliverance that came to the people of God.

Each of us owes much to parents and friends and neighbors and Sunday school teachers and youth leaders and pastors and evangelists and others who saw some potential in us and were willing to bear with our faults and give of themselves so that we could learn the ways of God. Let us always be thankful for such people, and let us show them our appreciation. Let us pray for them, and let us emulate their life of faith. Thank God for Amram and Jochebed. May more of us be like them.

If Amram and Jochebed could overcome in their time, then you, too, can face the seemingly impossible situations of your daily life and overcome. Say with me and say it with faith, *"I Can Do This!"*

Now, go out and do it in Jesus' name.

CHAPTER 12

MOSES: REFUSING TO BE IDENTIFIED WITH EGYPT

It was by faith that Moses, when he grew up, refused to be treated as the son of Pharaoh's daughter. He chose to share the oppression of God's people instead of enjoying the fleeting pleasures of sin. He thought it was better to suffer for the sake of the Messiah than to own the treasures of Egypt, for he was looking ahead to the great reward that God would give him. It was by faith that Moses left the land of Egypt. He was not afraid of the king. Moses kept right on going because he kept his eyes on the one who is invisible. It was by faith that Moses commanded the people of Israel to keep the Passover and to sprinkle blood on the doorposts so that the angel of death would not kill their firstborn sons. It was by faith that the people of Israel went right through the Red Sea as though they were on dry ground. But when the Egyptians followed, they were all drowned. Hebrews 11:24-29

It is one thing to have godly parents, but it is another thing entirely to accept the example of those godly parents and build upon it. And this is what Moses did.

Not every person of faith has children of faith, or even spiritual children. As a general rule, however, faith begets faith; and more often than not, those who have faith influence others around them to a life of faith as well. But faith is a very personal thing, and each of us must demonstrate his own faith in God. We noted earlier in the book the popular saying: "God has no grandchildren." It's all too true.

The faith of Moses is demonstrated in four great events: a decision, a journey, a celebration and a crossing.

THE DECISION

By faith Moses, when he was come to years, refused to be called the son of Pharaoh's daughter; choosing rather to suffer affliction with the people of God, than to enjoy the pleasures of sin for a season; esteeming the reproach of Christ greater riches than the treasures in Egypt: for he had respect unto the recompence of the reward. Hebrews 11:24-26, KJV

Moses was now grown and able to think for himself. He had been living in the palace of the Pharaoh and had been receiving the best education Egypt had to offer at the time. In fact, the Scriptures say of him:

Moses was taught all the wisdom of the Egyptians, and he became mighty in both speech and action.

Acts 7:22

Moses was now his own man, and it would not have been uncommon for him to lightly toss aside his mother's teachings. Young people do it every day, especially when they're influenced by a strong secular education. Somehow young people imagine that they know much more than the previous generation, that they're much wiser and can accomplish much more. In a measure, they're right. Each generation, with its accumulated wisdom, experience, and prosperity, should find itself a little further along the road to success than the previous generation. There would be nothing

It is one thing to have godly parents, but it is another thing entirely to accept the example of those godly parents and build upon it!

133

wrong in that, but it's not automatic. If young people make the wrong decisions in life, they quickly squander all the progress of past generations and fall back into the mire.

Each individual ultimately stands or falls on his own, and that standing or falling may depend on a few key decisions. Moses was faced with such a decision in his early adult life. He was, in a modern term, a dual national. He had two nationalities from which to choose, two distinct life-styles. If he accepted his adoption into the royal family, he would be in line to inherit the throne of the great Egyptian Empire and might someday become the most powerful and respected man on Earth (since apparently the Pharaoh had no male heir). If he made that decision, Moses would live in the palace, have all the best material things life had to offer and be waited on hand and foot.

The other alternative was to return to his Hebrew family. If he did that, he would live in a hut without the benefit of modern conveniences and be treated as a slave, without remuneration, or even thanks, for his efforts. He would have to take off his royal tunics and put on the raggedy garments that were the only thing available to the Hebrews. He would have to leave the special food of the palace, to which he had become accustomed, and return to the meager slave diet.

What a choice! What an alternative! Few of us would have had any difficulty at all making such a decision. The right choice seems obvious. And the sad truth is that most of us make our decisions in life based on expected monetary rewards or other material benefits and not on any spiritual consideration.

Money as a Motivator:

We can think of a thousand reasons to justify our decisions when there's money involved. Money has become the greatest motivator of our modern time, and this has probably been true of every generation. This is genuinely sad, because money is not a proper motivation for decision-making and often leads us to the wrong choice and to ultimate tragedy.

Moses had a serious choice to make. Which life-style would you have chosen? In the end, Moses *"refused to be called the son of Pharaoh's daughter,"* and he did it *"by faith."*

Does having faith in God mean that we must give up the best things in life? Does having faith in God mean that we must suffer deprivation and hardship? Does having faith in God mean that we must lose all the good things we might otherwise have? Absolutely not! Faith means trusting God to know what is best for us at any given moment.

Egypt was alluring, but it represented bondage to sin. The thought of returning to Goshen must have been abhorrent to Moses, but his decision was not based on which house was better or who served the best meals. It was a decision about his long-term spiritual welfare and the good of his people.

Satan often tries to portray life's great decisions in

terms of dollars and cents, but this is a deception. Moses was not choosing between riches and poverty; he was choosing between faith and paganism; he was choosing between the true and living God and some sun god, between truth and error, between good and evil. He knew his parents were right, and therefore he refused to deny their faith. Instead of denying it, he made it his own. To accept Ms. Pharaoh as his mother would have been to reject his real mother, and he could not bring himself to do that, whatever the consequences.

> *Both the sufferings associated with being a believer and the joys associated with being a sinner are temporary!*

Moses had learned something that every modern-day Christian needs to learn: both the sufferings associated with being a believer and the joys associated with being a sinner are temporary: *"Choosing rather to suffer affliction with the people of God, than to enjoy the pleasures of sin for a season."* There is always a measure of reproach associated with displaying faith in God. Others may not understand the life of faith and might try to denigrate it in some way. But any and all affliction associated with our faith is only a temporary thing. Our ultimate end is happiness and prosperity. We are destined for glory. Anything else is momentary, and no one and nothing can change this fact. Paul wrote to the early Church:

For I reckon that the sufferings of this present time are *not worthy* to be compared *with the glory which shall be revealed in us.* Romans 8:18

In the same way, any joy associated with the life of sin is also momentary. Life's delicacies, life's carnal pleasures, life's fleshly rewards are all fleeting. Afterward comes condemnation and punishment, and no one and nothing can change this fact.

Rich people are not necessarily happy people, and powerful people are not necessarily happy either. Happiness comes only from God. In fact, Moses was thinking correctly: *"Esteeming the reproach of Christ greater riches than the treasures in Egypt: for he had respect unto the recompence of the reward."*

The Treasures of Egypt:

What were these *"treasures of Egypt?"* Some of those treasures are kept in museums around the world today, and they are magnificent. Some of the most famous structures and some of the most famous and valuable artifacts ever discovered anywhere in the entire world have been found in Egyptian tombs and are related, for the most part, to the times of the Pharaohs. In their tombs, some gold-covered coffins, or sarcophagi, were discovered inside other, still larger gold-covered coffins, inside other, larger gold-covered coffins. And what we are now privileged to see represents only a small part of the treasures that existed in Moses' time.

As Pharaoh's grandson, no doubt Moses visited the treasure houses and saw room after gigantic room filled with gold and silver, jewels of all types, costly spices and regal garments. All of it could have been his—if he had been willing to denounce his Hebrew heritage. Moses refused, for he knew that there were greater riches in serving Christ than could be found in all the storehouses of Egypt.

The wording of this verse is interesting, for Moses lived several thousand years before the birth of Jesus. The fact that Christ is mentioned makes us know that Moses, like Abraham, Isaac, Jacob and Joseph before him, had a vision of things to come. As Moses would lead the children of Israel out of bondage in Egypt, Messiah would come to lead His people out of the bondage of sin. This revelation enabled Moses to decide the matter.

Moses was able to make a proper decision, even when the material and monetary pendulum had swung so far the other way, because he had his eyes upon the ultimate goal—a great secret that every believer must learn. If we take our eyes off of the prize, we are doomed to fail. When the goal is always in sight, we shall surely succeed.

THE JOURNEY

By faith he forsook Egypt, not fearing the wrath of the king: for he endured, as seeing him who is invisible.
Hebrews 11:27, KJV

It would have been very easy for Moses to turn back from his decision to identify with the hated Hebrews, for when he tried to help them, they rejected him. They resented his life of privilege and were suspicious of his intentions. And who could blame them? After all, Moses dressed as an Egyptian, spoke like an Egyptian and acted like an Egyptian. Moses did not, however, choose to use this initial rejection by his people as an excuse to turn back from his goal. He was determined to be faithful to God and to His people, and this decision led to a series of events that, instead, cut him off from Pharaoh and his possible inheritance.

What Motivated Moses?

A cursory reading of the Exodus account might leave one believing that Moses fled in fear of the Pharaoh:

But Moses fled from the face of Pharaoh, and dwelt in the land of Midian. Exodus 2:15, KJV

Similarly, when reading a second account of these events given by Stephen in early New Testament times and recorded in Acts 7, one might be led to believe that Moses fled because of the rejection he experienced when trying to help his people:

But he that did his neighbour wrong thrust him away, saying, Who made thee a ruler and a judge over us? Wilt thou kill me, as thou diddest the Egyptian yester-

*day? Then fled Moses at this saying, and was a stranger
in the land of Madian.* Acts 7:27-29, KJV

The truth, as expressed by Hebrews 11, is that Moses
fled *"by faith." "By faith he forsook Egypt."* What could this
mean? It must mean simply that he accepted his circumstances as being God's will for him at the time. He
needed time to seek God [He was forty years old when he
made this decision (see Acts 7:23 and 25)].

Something Had Taken Hold of His Heart:

What caused Moses to make this decision might be
referred to as a vision, a dream or a purpose. Something
had taken hold of his heart, and he would never be the
same again. Somehow he knew that he was responsible
for leading his people out of bondage. How this became
clear to him we don't know. Perhaps his mother had
planted the seeds of it in his heart many years before.
The important thing is that Moses knew, and he knew it
long before he saw the burning bush.

Others didn't understand the motivation of Moses,
and that is very typical and understandable. Receiving
such a vision from God is a rather lonely experience, because we often feel that we must convince everyone else
around us that what we're saying is, indeed, the will of
God, that it's possible and that we can achieve it. When
others fail to respond, as often happens, we must move
forward on our own, sometimes with the help and coop-
eration of only a few others, sometimes with just one

other person, and sometimes totally alone. It doesn't matter whether many or few cooperate with us in our calling. It only takes two people: myself and God. He knows exactly what He's doing, and He has called me to cooperate with it—whether others chose to do so or not.

Living as a "Stranger":

The same faith that had motivated and upheld his parents now kept Moses as he was forced to flee into the wilderness and wait for God's time to bring the people out of Egypt. He was accustomed to the easy life of the palace, but he now had to fend for himself in the wilderness. With each step, he proved God and His power, for he survived and moved forward. His experience is described in this short, but meaningful, phrase:

Others didn't understand the motivation of Moses, and that is very typical and understandable!

Moses ... was a stranger in the land of Madian.

Acts 7:29, KJV

Only someone who has lived as *"a stranger,"* a foreigner, in another land could fully understand the impact of those words. I know exactly what it means, for I, too, have been a "stranger" in many lands.

Moses Was Not Afraid of the King:

That Moses did not fear the most powerful man on Earth, as we have seen, is remarkable. Like his parents before him, He was able to avoid fearing Pharaoh because he feared God more. The fear of God frees us from all other fears and, therefore, sets us free to do God's will.

In the natural, Moses had reason to be fearful. Pharaoh was furious because Moses had spurned the years of special favor heaped upon him by the royal family (despite the fact that he was one of the despised Hebrews). How could he be so ungrateful? How could he betray his Egyptian family? He must not be allowed to live and get away with this.

During the years to come, a normal man would have been constantly looking over his shoulder, wondering if this would be the day the agents of Pharaoh would finally catch up with him. Moses, however, was a man of faith, a man of purpose, a man of destiny. He did not live his life in fear, but in hope. In this way, Moses lived forty more years in a period of intense preparation for what was to come.

THE CELEBRATION

Through faith he kept the passover, and the sprinkling of blood, lest he that destroyed the firstborn should touch them. Hebrews 11:28, KJV

God had not forgotten His promise, and one day He

spoke to Moses to go back to Egypt, face the new Pharaoh and say, *"Let my people go"* (Exodus 5:1). Moses obeyed. Not surprisingly, Pharaoh was very reluctant to cooperate. His slaves were valuable to him. They had built many fine cities and were a source of constant revenue.

It became necessary for Moses to persist over a period of time and to believe God for miraculous signs to convince Pharaoh that he could not win this fight. Satan will never give up his charges without a fight. But if we are persistent, we always win, for God is on our side.

God sent the plagues upon Egypt and upon the Egyptians, without affecting in any way the slaves of Goshen. And yet, with each plague, Pharaoh only seemed to harden his heart more. When Moses made his last visit to the Emperor, the man seemed more determined than ever to resist freeing the slaves and told Moses that he never wanted to see him again. If he tried to see him just one more time, he threatened, he would order him to be executed. Moses' answer is instructive:

> *Moses said, "You have spoken well. I will never see your face again."*   Exodus 10:29, NKJ

Clearly Pharaoh meant one thing by this, and Moses meant something entirely different.

Moses Was Not Intimidated:

Moses didn't seem to be troubled at all by Pharaoh's threats. Rather than become discouraged with the con-

> *This last plague would strike at the heart of every Egyptian home, killing the firstborn of every family — even the firstborn son of the Pharaoh!*

stant delaying tactics and the hardness of Pharaoh's heart, his faith had risen to a new height with each plague that God had sent, and now he knew something that Pharaoh did not know. He and his people would soon be departing from Egypt.

God had told the Israelites to borrow precious things from their Egyptian neighbors. The fact that the Egyptians were willing to loan anything at all to the Hebrews, let alone their most valuable possessions, shows the terror that existed in their hearts because of the plagues that had been visited upon them. They were becoming convinced that the best thing they could do would be to get rid of these foreigners—once and for all.

Only Pharaoh remained unconvinced, but God knew how to convince him. The final plague was revealed to Moses, the coming of the death angel. This last plague would strike at the heart of every Egyptian home, killing the first-born of every family—even the firstborn son of the Pharaoh. This blow would be so terrible, Moses predicted, that an unprecedented cry of anguish would rise up from the land:

Then a loud wail will be heard throughout the land of Egypt; there has never been such wailing before, and there never will be again. Exodus 11:6

Moses could be bold because he sensed that he would soon be departing—despite the threats of Pharaoh. When God has determined a thing, nothing and no one can stand in its way. The only thing that can prevent Him from fulfilling His purposes in our lives is our lack of faith.

Moses spoke boldly to Pharaoh of the coming, final, and terrible plague, and then he left the king's presence for the last time, feeling very excited that soon Pharaoh and his people would be begging him to leave Egypt.

It Was a New Day:

The next day Moses and Aaron told the Israelites some startling things. First, Moses said, they were beginning a new life and, therefore, would adopt the current month as the first month of their calendar. He was just that sure of what God was about to do.

Secondly, the people were to plan a very unusual celebration. This celebration would have a dual purpose. At the same time that they would be rejoicing in what God was about to do for them, they would also be protecting themselves from the tragedy that was about to be visited upon Egypt. Their celebration has come to be called Passover because the Death Angel passed over the houses of the Israelites, while bringing death and sadness to each Egyptian home.

In this first Passover celebration, the children of Israel were to do some very unusual things (see Exodus 12:3-13, KJV):

- Each household was to sacrifice a lamb.
- The lamb had to be male, young, and *"without blemish."*
- They were all to kill their lambs *"in the evening."*
- They were to take some of the blood of the sacrifice and put it on the sides and tops of the door frames of the houses where they would be gathered to eat some of the slain lamb.
- They were to roast their lamb (it could not be eaten any other way).
- That night they would eat the lamb together with *"unleavened bread"* and with *"bitter herbs."*

All of this was strange enough, but they were also instructed that they must eat everything. If anything was left till morning, it must be burned. They were to eat fully clothed, with their shoes on and a walking staff in one hand.

Finally, they were instructed:

Eat the food quickly [in haste, KJV], for this is the LORD's Passover. Exodus 12:11

That would have been far too much detail for most people: a certain kind of animal, prepared in a certain way at a certain time, the blood to be applied to the door posts, the dress code, the one-handed eating, the shoes, etc. ... these are just the sort of limitations our modern society rebels against, especially if one can see no logical reason for obeying and no personal gain involved. Moses explained at least one part of the plan to the Israelites:

The blood you have smeared on your doorposts will serve as a sign. When I see the blood, I will pass over you. This plague of death will not touch you when I strike the land of Egypt. Exodus 12:13

Perhaps this limited explanation was enough to ensure that the Israelites would obey God's commands. No other explanation was offered.

Acts of Faith in the Passover:

Looking back, thousands of years later, we understand that the Passover lamb represented Christ. His life was to be given. His body was to be sacrificed. His blood was to be shed to save mankind from sin and death and all its effects. That's why the Israelites had to offer a perfect sacrifice, and that's why their sacrifice had to be a lamb.

But could Moses and his people have understood these details one thousand, five hundred years before Christ? Probably not, for although animal sacrifice had been established very early, the details of Tabernacle and Temple sacrifice were yet to be defined. Moses was requiring the people to act in faith.

There were other acts of faith involved in the Passover celebration. Every laborer is anxious for the moment he or she can relax after a hard day's work and take off his or her shoes, but Moses told the people to eat fully dressed, with their shoes on and a staff in one hand. That is not an easy way to eat. By obeying God, the people were acting in faith that they would soon be starting on their journey.

Moses even spoke to them of coming generations, of establishing the Passover as a memorial for those coming generations and what each Jewish couple should tell their children and grandchildren when they celebrated Passover each successive year. These were all acts of faith. Many people, in this same situation, would have been preparing to die, but Moses was preparing to live. The Israelites must be ready to leave Egypt at sunrise the next morning.

Obeying Leadership without Needing To Understand Everything:

Moses could not have understood all the significance of what he was doing and asking others to do, but he obeyed—without understanding. And the rest of the children of Israel could not have understood the whys of what they were being asked to do that night. Perhaps they obeyed because of their confidence in Moses. That's not a bad reason for acting. When God has given us strong leadership, we can cooperate with that leadership with confidence, even if we sometimes have to do it without understanding. Faith is not understanding; it is obeying—whether we understand or not.

> *Moses could not have understood all the significance of what he was doing and asking others to do!*

If everyone had understood what God was saying, all of the Egyptians would have done exactly the same thing, and all of them would have been saved as well. Naaman didn't understand why he was being asked to dip seven times in the muddy Jordan River. Moses hadn't understood why God had told him to pick up a serpent on the back side of the desert. Joshua wouldn't understand why he was told to march around the walls of Jericho and say nothing. Gideon wouldn't understand why he was told to blow trumpets instead of taking military action. Elisha wouldn't be sure why he was instructed to tell the armies of Israel to *"make this valley full of ditches"* (2 Kings 3:16). God is looking for people who will trust Him, trust that He knows what He is doing, trust that He loves us and is working for our good, trust that obeying Him will always bring about a good result. That is simple faith: *"By faith, Moses kept the Passover,"* and the rest of the children of Israel joined him in this act of faith.

THE CROSSING

By faith they passed through the Red sea as by dry land: which the Egyptians assaying to do were drowned.   Hebrews 11:29, KJV

The Red Sea served two purposes. It was a means of destroying the armies of Pharaoh, but it was also a test of the faith of Moses and the people of Israel. Just as we all do, they would meet such tests constantly as they marched toward their Promised Land. It may seem unusual to think that people who had faced down the Pharaoh and who had seen God's hand at work in the plagues that eventually led to their deliverance would need further testing, but people change, especially as their circumstances change. Some people can serve God well in time of famine but are not able to do well when prosperity comes. Others are able to be true to God when things are going well, only to lapse into depression when things don't seem to go their way.

The people of Israel were facing new challenges. Life in the wilderness lacked security and frequently they thought of "home." The little they had possessed in Egypt suddenly seemed wonderful compared to facing another day of uncertainty in the wilderness. They sometimes forgot that they were marching toward a wonderful Promised Land and away from bondage in Egypt. As a result, the great majority of Israel's people failed the Red Sea test and even turned against Moses:

> As Pharaoh and his army approached, the people of Israel could see them in the distance, marching toward them. The people began to panic, and they cried out to the LORD for help. Then they turned against Moses and complained, "Why did you bring us out here to die in the wilderness? Weren't there enough graves for us in Egypt? Why did you make us leave? Didn't we tell you to leave us alone while we were still in Egypt? Our Egyptian slavery was far better than dying out here in the wilderness!"   Exodus 14:10-12

At first, Moses seemed to be firm in his own faith, but the constant murmuring and complaining of the people eventually affected him too. And, when it happened, God had to speak harshly to him, telling him to go forward. Apparently even Moses had entertained thoughts of going back.

God promised Moses that he would be avenged of the Egyptians:

> I will receive great glory at the expense of Pharaoh and his armies, chariots, and charioteers. When I am finished with Pharaoh and his army, all Egypt will know that I am the LORD!   Exodus 14:17-18

> *The Israelites made crossing the sea look so easy that the Egyptians tried to do the same thing, but when they did, they were all drowned!*

Next, God gave the children of Israel a sign that strengthened Moses' faith. A *"pillar of cloud"* (Exodus 13:21) suddenly moved between the camp of the Israelites and the pursuing Egyptians. To the Egyptians, it brought sudden darkness, while to the Israelites it provided light the entire night. Moses was so encouraged by this sign from God that he became willing to do the strange thing that God had told him to do. He stretched out his rod over the sea and held it there. As he did, God sent a mysterious wind that began to push back the waters of the Red Sea into a wall on each side. The next morning the children of Israel awoke to find a path of dry land across the sea, and they walked across *"on dry ground"* (Exodus 14:22).

The Israelites made crossing the sea look so easy that the Egyptians tried to do the same thing, but when they did, they were all drowned. The walls of water that had formed to open the sea fell in on them as they crossed. The Israelites watched as, within a few moments, the chariots and horses and soldiers of Pharaoh's army were totally destroyed. Not even one escaped. We can imagine that the faith of the children of Israel was certainly high that day. The Scriptures record:

> *This was how the LORD rescued Israel from the Egyptians that day. And the Israelites could see the bodies of the Egyptians washed up on the shore. When the people of Israel saw the mighty power that the LORD had displayed against the Egyptians, they feared the LORD and put their faith in him and his servant Moses.* Exodus 14:30-31

Now they *"believed the LORD"* (KJV). The trick is to believe Him always, whether we see the end from the beginning or not.

Their Trials Were Just Beginning:

Moses and the children of Israel were now on the other side of the Red Sea, but their trials were just beginning. In the coming years they would face physical need, danger from enemies they passed along the way, dissension in the ranks and change after change after change in their physical circumstances. You would think that after the experience of the Red Sea, these people would never doubt again, but it was not to be so. In circumstance after circumstance, Moses would be compelled to assure the people that disaster was not imminent, that God was still with them and that they should not turn back but, rather, keep moving forward toward the goal—the Promised Land.

It was hard for many of them to give up their slave mentality. They kept thinking about those simple fires outside their huts in Goshen where they had roasted leeks and garlic and whatever other meager foods that were allowed them, and those thoughts made them actually long to go back. Their desire to go back became so powerful that the generation that left Egypt was, in the end, not permitted to enter the Promised Land. After wandering for forty years in the wilderness, they died without ever allowing God to give them what He had promised.

Understanding Our Trials:

If we are to live successfully for our God, we must understand the trials of our faith. God never intends for any trial to do us harm, to make us fall, to rob us of joy or to cause us to go backward. His Word declares:

> *And we know that ALL THINGS work together for good to them that love God, to them who are the called according to his purpose.* Romans 8:28, KJV

When God says that *"all things work together"* for our good, what does He mean? He means all trials, all tests, all temptations, all hardships and all persecution. *All* means everything. It leaves nothing out. Therefore when we react negatively in times of trial, it reveals a lack of faith on our part. Tests are necessary and should be welcomed. A test should inspire joy in us, while we await the victory God will surely bring us through that test. In the meantime, we will stretch out our rod over the water, dig the valley full of ditches, march around the walls seven times or do whatever other unusual thing God commands us, for we trust His wisdom.

Whatever we do, we must never think of turning back. Our cry must be "Forward! Forward to the battle! Forward to the Promise Land! Egypt holds nothing for us." Let us learn from this great man, Moses, so that we don't miss our own Promised Land.

If Moses could overcome in his day, you, too, can face the seemingly impossible situations of your daily life and overcome. Say with me right now, and say it with faith, "*I Can Do This!*"

Now, go out and do it in Jesus' name.

CHAPTER 13

JOSHUA: MARCHING AROUND JERICHO

It was by faith that the people of Israel marched around Jericho seven days, and the walls came crashing down. Hebrews 11:30

According to modern archaeologists, Jericho is one of the oldest existing cities in the world. In Joshua's day, it was a fortress city, set in place to protect the boundaries of Canaan. The city had thick walls of stone, strong guard towers and gates, and was guarded constantly by well-armed soldiers. Still, it was the city God told His people to take first in their quest for the Promised Land. That may not have made sense to them at the time, but God always knows what He's doing.

COUNT IT AS DONE

The children of Israel had picked up some military experience on the other side of Jordan and had some weapons they had captured from their enemies, but they were certainly no match for Jericho. Still, God spoke to Joshua and said:

Joshua not only accepted God's word of faith (spoken in the past perfect tense), but he went on to repeat it himself!

I have given you Jericho, its king, and all its mighty warriors.
                    Joshua 6:2

This verb form *"have given"* is what is known in English grammar as past perfect tense. When God spoke to Joshua about taking the city of Jericho, He didn't speak of what might be in the future, but of what He had already done. Faith brings things out of the realm of mere possibility and into the realm of present reality. What God promises is so sure that we can say it is done and not be lying. God cannot fail, and He will not fail. Faith, therefore, allows us to express in the past tense things that are yet to come, as if they had already taken place. We can say it is done because we know that God will do it. He said so, and that is enough.

Few would argue that God has the right to count something done before it can be seen with the natural eye—if He wants to do that—but is it right for mortal men to do the same thing? To many, this is "stretching things," it is "borderline lying," it is "going a bit too far." The book of Hebrews, however, applauds the way Joshua took Jericho. He not only accepted God's word of faith (spoken in the past perfect tense), but he went on to repeat it himself and others:

> *The seventh time around, as the priests sounded the long blast on their horns, Joshua commanded the people, "Shout! For the* LORD *has given you the city!"*
>
> Joshua 6:16

God said, *"I have given you the city,"* and Joshua said, *"The* LORD *has given you the city."* And what's wrong with that? Why can't we say what God says? If He says it, we can say the same thing. Instead of saying what we think, what we imagine and what we feel, let's start saying what God says.

What I think may or may not be valid, what I imagine is often in error, and what I feel may be influenced by something I have experienced. But when God speaks, nothing can change His will or His word, and I can count on it bearing fruit.

When Joshua spoke these words of faith, nothing had changed. The sturdy walls and gates of Jericho stood as before. The guards were in their places, vigilant and fear-some looking. The city was shut up tight and ready for a long siege. But when God has spoken, nothing else matters. Whatever the circumstances, we can be sure that He will work for us, and we can boldly say, *"God has given us the city."* We can even start thanking God for the victory long before we see it come to pass. Indeed, faith demands that we praise Him in advance.

COMPLETE VICTORY DEPENDS ON COMPLETE OBEDIENCE

Complete victory, however, depends upon complete obedience: *"The walls of Jericho fell down, after they were compassed about seven days"* (KJV). It didn't happen before Joshua had done everything God told him to do, and it didn't happen while he was doing what God had told him to do. It only happened *"after"* he had done all that God had told him to do.

What God does for us is usually done in this coopera-tive way. His work is a cooperative effort, and He allows us to participate in the miracle. He does the miracle, but we must do something to bring it about. What we do seems to trigger what has already been determined by God.

Some have the idea that faith is just snapping our fin-gers and telling God what to do for us, but He's not our slave to be ordered around at our whim. Faith is first find-ing out what God wants in a given situation (not what I want) and then obeying Him in every detail of how He tells me to go about laying the groundwork for the miracle. If I believe Him and obey Him, He never fails to do what He has promised.

But it doesn't happen before I obey Him, it doesn't happen when I start obeying Him, it only happens when I have completely obeyed Him. So I can't get discouraged and give up halfway through the process. I must obey God fully in order to receive the completed miracle. At Jericho, absolutely nothing happened until the children of Israel had obeyed completely.

THE ALL-IMPORTANT DETAILS

Joshua told the people what God had ordered them to do. They were to march around the city walls once each day for six days. The most prominent part of the procession would be made up of seven priests bearing trumpets. They would blow these trumpets as they marched, while behind them would come the Ark of the Covenant. One guard contingency would go before the priests and the Ark, and another would come behind. The rest of the people would follow.

Aside from the blowing of the seven trumpets, there was to be no sound for the first six days:

"Do not shout; do not even talk," Joshua commanded. "Not a single word from any of you until I tell you to shout. Then shout!" Joshua 6:10

On the seventh day, they were to march around the

walls seven times. After the seventh time, the trumpets would sound, and all the people would join in a great shout. If they did all this, God promised, the walls would fall down flat before them, and they could go in and take the city without a fight.

THE MARCH BEGAN

The march began with great anticipation, and everything went according to schedule:

> *So the Ark of the Lord was carried around the city once that day, and then everyone returned to spend the night in the camp.* Joshua 6:11

I can imagine that there were more than a few who were disappointed after the first day of marching was completed with a total lack of visible results. They must have wondered if they were really doing the right thing. There are always a few who tire easily and early and think that they know a better way of doing things. In fact, most Christians are results oriented and want to see something happen NOW. But, like it or not, God does things in His own time and in His own way. He is not rushed by our impatience, and He will not change His plan to accommodate our lack of understanding. Things get done His way, or they don't get done at all.

I can imagine that a few of Joshua's people came to him that night complaining that the enemy was making fun of them and asking what they could do differently the next time to avoid this reproach. Joshua was not moved by these complaints, and the next day they all embarked on another round of si-lent marching.

When two days went by and there was no visible change at all—no crack in the walls and no weakening of the courage of the guards stationed there—experience tells me that there were more com-plaints from the congregation. Why was nothing happening? Might there not be a better way to do this thing?

Perhaps they came in small groups to Joshua's tent to bring their suggestions about what was being done wrong. Was he sure about all the details? Perhaps the Ark should go first, then the trumpets, then the guard. This second-guessing must have in-creased daily, as they finished their march and saw no results whatsoever.

> *There are always a few who tire easily and early and think that they know a better way of doing things!*

AFTER SEVERAL DAYS

After several days, some must have begun calling the whole thing "ridiculous" and suggesting some possible military solution. If nothing was happening, and that seemed apparent to everyone, shouldn't they try another tactic? They could be marching like this for the rest of their lives, and they might die marching around Jericho, just as their fathers had died on the other side of the Jordan.

By the fourth and fifth times around, I'm sure that some were ready to give up. They would have concluded that Joshua was not a good leader. How could anyone have expected him to fill the enormous shoes of Moses? Anyone and everyone knew that was impossible! Joshua's ideas didn't seem to be practical because they were producing nothing of substance.

JOSHUA'S CHALLENGE

This undercurrent of disquiet must have increased daily. How Joshua quelled it we don't know, but surely he just repeated each evening exactly what God had told him. What else could he say? I can imagine his exhortation:

"God said that if we would march around the city once each day for the first six days and seven times on the seventh day, He would do the work. And we must trust Him. He will not fail us. Let us obey Him fully and give Him a chance to prove Himself to us."

"Some of you have excellent suggestions about the order of the march, but God told us where to place the Ark in the order of procession. Some of you are bothered by the silence, but God Himself told us to hold our peace until the end of the seventh day. Let us be faithful to Him and see what He will then do for us."

Since the people had not talked directly to the Lord, they had to rely on Joshua as God's mouthpiece. It is often in our failure to trust the leadership God has placed over us that we lose our battles. If our leaders prove to be untrustworthy, that's one thing, but if we're just too impatient and too rebellious to be cooperative with them, that's another. God is looking for people whom He can trust to act as a great army, to go forth and do exploits for Him as one man. Often, the Joshuas among us must go up and take life's Jerichos by themselves, because no one else will listen to them long enough to help them get the job done.

The challenge of a spiritual leader is to gain the trust of his or her people and to communicate in a clear and simple manner what it is that God has shown them. If we cannot communicate the vision and encourage others to cooperate in the execution of it, we're doomed to stand alone on life's battlefields.

At Jericho, nothing happened until the seventh day and the seventh time around the city. Nothing happened until Joshua and the children of Israel completely obeyed. It is often at this critical point that Satan attacks us most fiercely and tries desperately to turn us around and keep us from the final victory. How many times are we nearing the point of victory, only to give up and miss what God has promised us?

THE WALLS COLLAPSED

Upon complete obedience, *"the wall collapsed [fell down flat,* KJV] (Joshua 6:20)—just as the Lord had promised. Why do we ever doubt? Has God failed us even once? He gave Abraham and Sarah a child, just as He had promised. He caused Joseph to reign over his brothers, just as He had promised. He caused water to fall from the sky upon the people of Noah's generation, just as He had promised. God never fails. He is totally and absolutely reliable. He is worthy of our trust, worthy of our confidence, worthy of our faith. Believe Him and obey Him, for complete obedience, motivated by faith, always brings complete victory. Learn from Joshua's example.

If Joshua could overcome in his day, then you, too, can face the seemingly impossible situations of your daily life and overcome. Say with me right now, and say it with faith, *"I Can Do This!"*

Now, go out and do it in Jesus' name.

CHAPTER 14

RAHAB:
WELCOMING THE SPIES

It was by faith that Rahab the prostitute did not die with all the others in her city who refused to obey God. For she had given a friendly welcome to the spies.   Hebrews 11:31

This woman named Rahab is clearly identified in the Scriptures as a *"prostitute, (harlot, KJV)."* Isn't that interesting? If God were only looking for perfect people, He never would have found any. Although the Bible uses the word "perfect" in relationship to several of its major characters, other things we read about those same characters show us that they were not so perfect—in our manner of measuring perfection at least. Still, as we have seen, the negative aspects of their lives were never hidden from us. They are there for us all to see.

SIN, BEFORE OR AFTER KNOWING CHRIST

Some Bible characters who sinned grievously did so before they knew God, as in the case of Rahab. Others, however, sinned later in life—when they should have known better. Among them were Abraham, David and Peter. If God had hid from our eyes the imperfections of these saints, we might all despair and think that because we are far from perfect ourselves, these same blessings could never be for us. But God is clearly not looking for perfect people; He is looking for imperfect people whom He can perfect.

The revelation that Rahab was a prostitute only reminds us of the great mercy of our God and His power to change lives. Sin is not a problem for God. He knows how to deal with it, and He does so with great ease and compassion. All He asks in return is that we recognize our call to a new life and make every effort to walk in that newness.

JUSTIFIED BY WORKS

Aside from being a prostitute, Rahab was also a pagan woman, one who did not know God. When she met the spies whom Joshua had sent to Jericho, she was impressed with them and with their faith. In the short time they were in Jericho, she could not have possibly learned everything there was to learn about God, but she liked what she saw and heard and was willing to act on it—putting her own life at risk to save these godly men.

In his lesson on faith without works, James teaches us that Rahab was *"justified by works, when she had received the messengers"* (James 2:25, KJV). Something inspired this woman to action, and what she did was something that many "good" people would have hesitated to do.

Of all the people of Jericho, only Rahab willingly received the spies. When the king of Jericho learned that the spies were in her house, he sent for them. Rahab, because of her fear of God, protected them, hiding them and helping them to escape. Why would she do that? Why would she risk her life to save men whom she had only recently met and about whom she knew so little? The stories of faith she had been hearing were taking hold of her heart.

> *If God had hid from our eyes the imperfections of these saints, we might all despair and think that ... these same blessings could never be for us!*

I Can Do This!

FAITH RISING

When things had quieted down in the city and soldiers had called off their search for the two spies (who were even then hiding under some flax on Rahab's rooftop), she went up to them and said some very amazing things:

> "I know the LORD has given you this land," she told them. "We are all afraid of you. Everyone is living in terror. For we have heard how the LORD made a dry path for you through the Red Sea when you left Egypt. And we know what you did to Sihon and Og, the two Amorite kings east of the Jordan River, whose people you completely destroyed. No wonder our hearts have melted in fear! No one has the courage to fight after hearing such things. For the LORD your God is the supreme God of the heavens above and the earth below."
>
> Joshua 2:9-11

This woman had somehow received the same faith that came to Joshua. She was speaking of the conquest of Jericho in the past perfect tense: *"I know the LORD has given you this land."* All the people of Jericho had heard the very same stories Rahab had heard—the plagues of Egypt and the resulting escape from slavery, the crossing of the Red Sea and the conquest of the kings on the other side of Jordan—but, among all those who had heard, only this woman believed.

Perhaps Rahab was not converted by the spies; perhaps she had been converted for some time already. When she had first heard the stories of God's power, perhaps her heart had been strangely warmed, and she had realized that this was He whom she had been seeking all her life. Her reception of the spies was probably not a spur-of-the-moment decision. She may have been praying for a very long time about how she could help these people.

Her neighbors surely had heard the same accounts, but they dismissed them. Why did Rahab react differently? She truly believed that this powerful God (of Whom she had heard so much) would do exactly what He had promised, and she wanted to be part of it. There were many gods in Canaan, but she had decided long ago: *"the LORD your God is the supreme God of the heavens above and the earth below."*

REMEMBER ME

Rahab was so sure of what God was going to do that she now asked the spies to remember her when they came back to take the city. There was no doubt in her mind that they would do just that. She had become willing to disobey her own king, for she had learned that there was a higher authority, the King of Heaven, and she had decided to cast her lot with Him and those who served Him.

A signal was given to her, a signal which she would use when receiving the victors of the coming battle. She must tie a scarlet chord across her window. Her neighbors, no doubt, thought she was signalling that she was back in business, but instead she was declaring to the conquering Israelites that she was one of them.

Rahab became a follower of Jehovah, married a servant of the Lord, and became an ancestor of the Lord Jesus Christ!

Only those who were found in the house with the scarlet thread would be spared. So if Rahab wanted her parents and her brothers and sisters to be saved, she would have to bring them all into her house and keep them there. Anyone who wandered out into the streets would be on his own, but anyone who remained behind the scarlet thread would be saved. Rahab carefully obeyed the instructions of the Hebrew spies.

It must have been very encouraging for Joshua to know that a woman of Jericho had confirmed everything that God had told him and that a family was waiting, behind closed doors, to join his people once the battle was over. Rahab's faith also encouraged the spies and saved their lives. Not only did she hide them in her house and lower them down from the city wall when it was safe, but she told them where to hide for the next few days while the furor over their presence in the area subsided.

SAVING HERSELF

In saving the spies, Rahab saved herself, for Joshua gave strict orders to all his people not to let any harm come to her:

The city and everything in it must be completely destroyed as an offering to the LORD. Only Rahab the prostitute and the others in her house will be spared, for she protected our spies. Joshua 6:17

When that great shout went up on the eve of the seventh day, the walls of Jericho fell flat, and the Israelites stormed into the city to plunder and burn it. Two men were sent by Joshua on a special mission. They moved past street battles, searching for a house with a scarlet thread tied in the window. When they found it, they brought out to safety all of its occupants—Rahab, her parents, and her brothers and sisters—and escorted them to a safe place outside the city.

The title prostitute would be one that Rahab could spend many years shaking off, but she never returned to her profession. She became a follower of Jehovah, married a servant of the Lord, and became an ancestor of our Lord Jesus Christ (see Matthew 1:5-6). We have much to learn from this noble woman of faith.

If Rahab could overcome in her day, then you, too, can face the seemingly impossible situations of your daily life and overcome. Say with me right now, and say it with faith, *"I Can Do This!"*

Now, go out and do it in Jesus' name.

CHAPTER 15

HOW MUCH MORE DO I NEED TO SAY?

Well, how much more do I need to say? It would take too long to recount the stories of the faith of Gideon, Barak, Samson, Jephthah, David, Samuel, and all the prophets. By faith these people overthrew kingdoms, ruled with justice, and received what God had promised them. They shut the mouths of lions, quenched the flames of fire, and escaped death by the edge of the sword. Their weakness was turned to strength. They became strong in battle and put whole armies to flight. Women received their loved ones back again from death. But others trusted God and were tortured, preferring to die rather than turn from God and be free. They placed their hope in the resurrection to a better life.

Some were mocked, and their backs were cut open with whips. Others were chained in dungeons. Some died by stoning, and some were sawed in half; others were killed with the sword. Some went about in skins of sheep and goats, hungry and oppressed and mistreated. They were too good for this world. They wandered over deserts and mountains, hiding in caves and holes in the ground.

Hebrews 11:32-38

The first battle that Gideon had to fight, however, was not against the Midianites, but against his own doubts!

What a long and grand P.S.! It began with these words: *"Well, how much more do I need to say? It would take too long ..."* As with every letter, there was a limit to what could be said in this one, and the writer, after applauding the faith of Abel, Enoch, Noah, Abraham, Isaac, Sarah, Jacob, Joseph, Amram and Jochebed, Moses, Joshua and Rahab—an amazing undertaking in just one chapter— ran out of space and time. He could not, however, finish his letter without mentioning others of the truly great men and women of faith: Gideon, Barak, Samson, Jephthah, David, Samuel, and *"all the prophets."* Although not every great man and woman of faith could be named in such a short list, we can learn much from those whom the writer does include. Let us briefly look at these before exploring the most important point of this book: how to exercise faith for your own daily needs and challenges.

Gideon: Raising an Army

Well, how much more do I need to say? It would take too long to recount the stories of the faith of Gideon.

Hebrews 11:32

Gideon's experience was similar, in many ways, to that of Joshua at Jericho. God chose Gideon to lead the armies of Israel into battle against an enemy, God gave him specific and unusual instructions to carry out, and his victory depended on obedience to those detailed instructions. The first battle that Gideon had to fight, however, was not against the Midianites, but against his own doubts. Why would God call him, he reasoned, when he was from a poor family and was the least important member of that family? Some of that may have been modesty, but Gideon did indeed have a fear problem, one that had to be overcome—if he was to excel in God.

God Was Patient with Gideon:

God was patient with Gideon. First He sent an angel to visit the young man and to call him to this work. Next He answered the "fleece" Gideon put forth, and He did it without question or comment. Then, when Gideon had

called the people to battle and was still setting forth
"fleeces," God answered him each time, with no com-
plaint.

When Gideon seemed convinced that God was about
to give his army victory, he was instructed to proceed to a
place known as Harod. *Harod* means "trembling."
Gideon, apparently, wasn't the only one who was afraid.
Many of his soldiers were also fearful, and God showed
him how to weed out the most fearful from among them:

> *Therefore, tell the people, "Whoever is timid or afraid
> (fearful, KJV) may leave and go home." Twenty-two
> thousand of them went home, leaving only ten thou-
> sand who were willing to fight.*   Judges 7:3

There's no place in God's army for the fearful. The
fearful work against the true believers. Faith and doubt
will not mix any better than oil and water. *"The fearful"*
are consigned to a terrible end:

> *But the fearful, and unbelieving, and abominable, and
> murderers, and whoremongers, and sorcerers, and
> idolaters, and all liars, shall have their part in the lake
> which burneth with fire and brimstone: which is the
> second death.*   Revelation 21:8, KJV

God is looking for men of faith, and the fearful must
be eliminated. In one single stroke, Gideon lost two-
thirds of his troops. The Lord assured him, however, that

he could do more with ten thousand men who believed the promise of God than with the larger troop of thirty-two thousand.

A Second Test:

When God showed Gideon a second test of his soldiers (a test some have interpreted as a test of readiness, alertness, or willingness), he lost another big chunk of his army. Still, Gideon was not discouraged because God had told him that the people were *"too many"* (Judges 7:4).

How could there be *"too many"* against an enemy so great? There were *"too many"* because God refuses to share His glory with another. He never wants us to say that we have overcome because of superior numbers, ability or human wisdom. What we do must be done in the Spirit and to the glory of God.

When the dust settled, only three hundred faithful men were left in Gideon's army. Still, the man of God was confident of victory. God had spoken to him, as He had to Joshua in an earlier time, in the past tense:

> *It happened on the same night that the Lord said to him, "Arise, go down against the camp, for I have delivered it into your hand."* Judges 7:9, NKJ

But God knew that there was still an element of fear left in Gideon, so He instructed him to accompany a servant to the enemy lines. There they overheard a Midianite talking about a strange dream, a dream the enemy interpreted as a sign that God would give

Gideon victory over them the following day. When Gideon heard that dream and its interpretation from the lips of a pagan, he was strengthened—as God had promised he would be—and he went forth to repeat God's promise to his fellow soldiers:

And so it was, when Gideon heard the telling of the dream and its interpretation, that he worshiped. He returned to the camp of Israel, and said, "Arise, for the Lord has delivered the camp of Midian into your hand."
Judges 7:15, NKJ

God understands human nature and is ready and willing to work with us so that we can overcome our fears and be strengthened in faith. By taking the leadership in the battle against the Midianites and winning, Gideon established himself among the people and became one of the early judges of the nation. Through faith, he had become that *"mighty man of valor"* the angel of the Lord had foreseen him to be.

BARAK: RECOGNIZING TRUE LEADERSHIP

Well, how much more do I need to say? It would take too long to recount the stories of the faith of ... Barak.
Hebrews 11:32

The appearance of Barak in the list of heroes is surprising only in the sense that very little is recorded about him in the Bible. He was a military leader under the judgeship of Deborah. He apparently had little exceptional personal leadership ability, for when it came time to go forth to battle, he was willing to go only if Deborah led the way:

Barak told her [Deborah], "I will go, but only if you go with me!"
Judges 4:8

This is a most interesting concept and proves that many times greatness lies in the ability to recognize leadership in others, to recognize a special anointing upon a person and the willingness to identify and cooperate with that anointing. Each of us must learn this secret and develop the habit of association with people of faith and power.

We see many examples of this in the Bible. For instance, because David became great, his servant Joab also became great. Joab was exalted only because he identified with a man of destiny (see 2 Samuel 2:13). Before David became king, he willingly submitted himself to the leadership of Saul (see 1

God understands human nature and is ready and willing to work with us so that we can overcome our fears and be strengthened in faith!

Samuel 16:19-21) and refused to lay a hand on Saul, even when the king was unusually cruel to him. Elisha achieved greatness by associating himself with Elijah and accepting him as his *"master"* (see 2 Kings 2:3, KJV). Joshua was able to lead the children of Israel into the Promised Land because of his long association with Moses (see Exodus 24:13, 33:11 and Joshua 1:1).

Barak's Willingness to Follow a Woman:

In the case of Barak and Deborah, there is a second element of importance to be found in his decision—the fact that he was willing to submit himself to the leadership of a woman. Indeed, he insisted upon it. If the woman was anointed of God, then he was ready to submit to her authority and give her the place of prominence. This is a rare quality in men and one worthy of praise, for God is truly *"no respecter of persons"* (Acts 10:34, KJV). Much of the teaching commonly put forth by the predominantly male leadership of the church about keeping everything in male hands is misplaced and generally not helpful. If God *"doesn't show partiality,"* then it's time that we, too, recognize what His Word has long declared:

> *There is neither Jew nor Greek, there is neither slave nor free, there is neither male nor female; for you are all one in Christ Jesus.* Galatians 3:28, NKJ

Why are we so slow to recognize this truth?

The Song of Deborah and Barak:

When Barak and Deborah had led their forces into

battle and succeeded in routing the armies of their enemies, a special song was sung, a song that has come to be known as *"the song of Deborah and Barak"* (Judges 5:2-31). The passage begins like this:

> *On that day Deborah and Barak son of Abinoam sang this song:*
>
> *"When Israel's leaders take charge,*
> *and the people gladly follow—*
> *bless the LORD!"*   Judges 5:1-2

The victory that day was for both Deborah (the first mentioned) and Barak (the man who recognized her leadership and followed it).

Some have called this song simply "The Song of Deborah," and that is technically correct, for without her there would have been no victory. But by recognizing God's hand upon Deborah and being willing to submit to her leadership, Barak also secured his place in the song. There are many individuals who are not exceptional leaders, but when they join themselves to anointed and chosen servants of God, they become very effective for His Kingdom.

Then There Was Peace in the Land:

It is worthy of note that the chapter which recorded the history of Barak ends with the notation:

> *Then there was peace in the land for forty years.*
>   Judges 5:31

When we have men of simple faith and obedience like Barak over us, we can live in rest and peace.

SAMSON: RECOVERING STRENGTH

Well, how much more do I need to say? It would take too long to recount the stories of the faith of ... Samson. Hebrews 11:32

Samson was a man of contradictions. He was separated as a Nazarite from birth (see Judges 13:5 and 16:17), yet he regularly kept bad company (14:1-3). At times, he was very spiritual (13:25 and 15:14), while at other times he was clearly dominated by carnal desires (16:1-4). He was a man of courage in battle (15:11-14), yet he showed childishness in the tactics he employed (15:11-14). He was physically strong (16:3, 9, 12 and 14), and yet he was morally weak (16:15-17). In the end, Samson's moral weaknesses caused his downfall, leaving him blinded, bound and forced to work like some farm animal for his captors.

> *Jephthah was an unlikely candidate for leadership!*

Fortunately Samson's story has a happy ending. The misery of slavery could not have been a pleasant one, but it led Samson to recognize his failure and to call upon God. In time, his strength was restored, and he was avenged of his enemies in death.

Samson, a man of simple faith, was judge over Israel for twenty years.

Jephthah: Keeping a Sacred Vow

Well, how much more do I need to say? It would take too long to recount the stories of the faith of ... Jephthah. Hebrews 11:32

Jephthah was an unlikely candidate for leadership. His mother was a prostitute (see Judges 11:1). He lived for a time in the house of his father, but his other siblings rejected him and eventually drove him away (verse 2). His neighbors agreed that this was the proper thing to do (verse 7). Jephthah soon found himself with the wrong crowd of people, whom the Bible calls *"vain men"* (verse 3, KJV). But God had a plan for Jephthah, and that plan developed over time.

For some reason, when the Ammonites started a war with Israel, the men of Gilead, the very men who had rejected Jephthah and had been glad when he was gone from their midst, now went in search of him. For some reason, they now wanted to make him their military leader. This is a very curious turn of events that leads us to believe that Jephthah had not been spending his time in bitterness and anger, but had somehow gotten his life turned around. The men of Gilead not only wanted Jephthah as their military commander; they also wanted him to judge their people.

Jephthah proved himself to be an able and knowledgeable negotiator. He had learned much through his own experience, but even more by talking regularly with God. He had come to recognize that God was the true Judge over Israel (see Judges 11:27). When the Ammonites did not respond favorably to his negotiation, he was moved by the Spirit of God to act against them militarily. He prevailed and, thus, kept the people of Israel free from their enemies.

The Fateful Vow:

Jephthah is remembered most, however, for a strong vow he made to God on the eve of his military foray:

> *And Jephthah made a vow to the* Lord. *He said, "If you give me victory over the Ammonites, I will give to the* Lord *the first thing coming out of my house to greet me when I return in triumph. I will sacrifice it as a burnt offering."*   Judges 11:30-31

It is not clear exactly what or whom Jephthah expected to see coming out from the door of his house when he returned, but since he spoke of a burnt offering, he must have been thinking about one of his animals and was contemplating how he would use it to give thanks to God for the victory over the Ammonites.

What is very clear is that Jephthah never expected his daughter, his only child, to be the first thing he would see coming through that door when he got home. When that precise thing happened, his reaction to this sad turn of events was understandable. He *"tore his clothes in anguish"* and cried out, *"My heart is breaking!"* We can only imagine what he was feeling in those moments.

Most of us would have understood if Jephthah had excused himself and not kept this particular vow. Although we know that vows are important and that it's *"better not to vow than to vow and not pay"* (Ecclesiastes 5:5, NKJ), this seems like an exceptional case. Jephthah, however, made no excuses. His response was:

> *I have made a vow to the L*ORD *and cannot take it back.*
>
> Judges 11:35

> *I have opened my mouth unto the L*ORD, *and I cannot go back.*
> Judges 11:35, KJV

That powerful statement demonstrates Jephthah's simple, yet profound, faith in God. He was sure that God knew what was best—even if he didn't understand what was happening at the moment. This enabled him to refuse to turn back.

The Daughter Agreed:

The daughter of Jephthah herself, when she knew what her father had promised God, agreed with him fully:

> *And she said, "Father, you have made a promise to the L*ORD. *You must do to me what you have promised, for the L*ORD *has given you a great victory over your enemies, the Ammonites.*
> Judges 11:36

This child had been well taught and recognized the need to honor a vow to God. She asked only to have some time before she was offered, and that request was, of course, granted.

What Was the Outcome?

In the case of Abraham offering up Isaac, God intervened at the last moment and presented another sacrifice. In the case of Jephthah and his daughter, we're left wondering exactly what did happen. The Scriptures say only:

> *When she returned home, her father kept his vow, and she died a virgin. So it has become a custom in Israel for young Israelite women to go away for four days each year to lament the fate of Jephthah's daughter.* Judges 11:39-40

This is one of the great question marks of the Bible, for we don't have any way of knowing what actually happened. What we can say is that Jephthah was remembered as a man of faith, that he kept his commitments to God and that he went on to judge Israel for six years after this incident. The rest we must leave with God. It seems inconceivable to me, personally, that God would require the sacrifice of a man's daughter, but who am I to judge the Almighty? He does all things well.

DAVID: BRINGING GREATNESS TO ISRAEL

Well, how much more do I need to say? It would take too long to recount the stories of the faith of ... David. Hebrews 11:32

David was one of the most important characters in the Bible. He had such an important place in the heart of God that when Jesus was born, He was called *"the Son of David"* (Matthew 1:1, KJV).

To What Can We Attribute David's Success?

David had a lot going for him. He excelled as athlete, musician, poet, soldier and king. His success, however, was not because of his age, for he was the youngest son of Jesse and, as such, was passed over during the visit of the prophet Samuel, when he had gone in search of Israel's next king.

Precisely because of his youth and inexperience, David was relegated to the lowly job of tending sheep!

David's success was not due to his experience. Precisely because of his youth and inexperience, he was relegated to the lowly job of tending sheep.

189

David's success was not due to his size. King Saul was a big man, but David was quite small in stature.

David's success was not due to his reputation, for he was well known only to his sheep. When Samuel called for other brothers to interview, the entire family seemed to forget for the moment that David even existed. He was little more than a last thought, as far as they were concerned.

David's success was due solely to his simple faith in God, a faith nurtured in the solitude of the sheepfold. It was there, and also in the quietness of the fields, that David talked to God and sang to Him and developed a style of worship and a body of psalms that have blessed the world ever since.

David Was Fearless:

When thrust into the arena of battle with Goliath (seemingly by accident), David was not afraid because God had been with him when he encountered a bear and, later, a lion. He had defeated both of them, and he knew that God would help him now. He was not adversely affected by the terror the soldiers in Israel's service were experiencing. He willingly faced the giant and won.

The call to service came very early in David's life, as it had in Joseph's, and, in the same way that Joseph had to wait patiently for thirteen years, while God molded him, David had to pass a similar period of test before he assumed the throne of Israel.

David refused to further his own cause by killing Saul, although he had at least two opportunities to do so. Who could have blamed him for killing a king who had turned against him for no apparent reason and began persecuting him mercilessly?

David's faith united and extended the kingdom of the Jews, and he secured for them a site that would become holy to the whole world—Jerusalem. When he took the Ark of the Covenant into that holy city, he did so with great rejoicing, with dancing and with sacrifices to God.

Much of what we know today about worship we have learned from David, who set up anointed musicians and singers to wait before the Lord and to bring the people into the presence of the Lord. The humble Tabernacle of David, probably nothing more than a tent, brought great glory to the Holy City and left its mark for all future generations.

David's Failures:

It was David who made preliminary preparations for the construction of the great Temple in Jerusalem, but he was forbidden to actually build it, because he had proven to be *"a man of war"* (1 Chronicles 28:3, KJV). David was apparently caught in the trap of his own authority, as commonly happens when men forget Who is in charge and, thus, forget to listen for Heaven's commands. It seems that David came to enjoy war and went beyond the bounds that God had set for him.

At one time, before becoming king, David led a group of malcontents. He numbered Israel, against God's wishes. He sinned with Bathsheba and complicated this failing by having her husband Uriah killed in battle.

But with all his failures, David was redeemed and kept his kingdom, while Saul lost his for a lesser infraction. This was because David was also a man of repentance. He sang:

Have mercy on me, O God,
because of your unfailing love.
Because of your great compassion,
blot out the stain of my sins.
Wash me clean from my guilt.
Purify me from my sin.
For I recognize my shameful deeds—
they haunt me day and night.
Against you, and you alone, have I sinned;
I have done what is evil in your sight.
You will be proved right in what you say,
and your judgment against me is just.
Purify me from my sins, and I will be clean;
wash me, and I will be whiter than snow.
Oh, give me back my joy again;
you have broken me—
now let me rejoice.
Don't keep looking at my sins.
Remove the stain of my guilt.
Create in me a clean heart, O God.

> **Despite his repentance and restoration, David suffered much for his sin!**

192

Renew a right spirit within me.
Do not banish me from your presence,
and don't take your Holy Spirit from me.
Restore to me again the joy of your salvation,
and make me willing to obey you.

Psalm 51:1-4 and 7-12

Because his heart was tender toward God, David was forgiven (see 2 Samuel 12:13).

Suffering for Sin:

Despite his repentance and restoration, David suffered much for his sin. His newborn son died; his son Amnon raped his sister Tamar; another son, Absalom, killed Amnon; Absalom later divided David's kingdom and forced his father to flee from his capital; then Joab, David's faithful servant, killed Absalom.

All in all, David had more than his share of personal problems, yet he prevailed in his faith and prepared Solomon to take his place and to build what he had been unable to build. History judged him well, and he became known as *"a man after [God's] own heart"* (1 Samuel 13:14). We can all learn much from such an example.

SAMUEL: REFUSING TO ALLOW ONE WORD TO DROP TO THE GROUND

Well, how much more do I need to say? It would take too long to recount the stories of the faith of ... Samuel.

Hebrews 11:32

Samuel was the last of the judges over Israel. He was blessed because he had a mother who loved God and who loved him. She accepted him as a miracle from God and consecrated him to the service of the Lord, even before he was born.

Living in the Temple:

Good to her word, just as soon as the boy was weaned (apparently much later than we wean our children these days), Hannah took Samuel to the Temple and left him there to be trained in the priesthood. This could have been a traumatic experience for a child so young, but Hannah never stopped loving Samuel and came each year to present him with a new coat.

What a privilege it was for Samuel to be able to minister to the Lord at such a young age! This experience helped him begin to hear God's voice and to eventually become a prophet to the nation.

Samuel responded to the favor of the Lord upon his life by not letting any of God's words *"fall to the ground"* (1 Samuel 3:19, KJV). Instead, he became a man of serious prayer and contemplation, boldly declaring to the nation all that which God revealed to him.

Samuel Had Many Firsts:

It was during Samuel's lifetime that Israel rebelled against God's form of government (theocracy) and insisted on having a king like other nations (monarchy). When this happened, Samuel wept before the Lord, but God comforted him, telling him that the people were not rejecting him personally; they were actually rejecting God. God then used Samuel to anoint the first two kings of Israel—first Saul and then, when Saul failed, David.

Samuel also established a school of the prophets, teaching other men the spiritual secrets he had learned himself.

Samuel was later considered to be the forerunner of all Jewish prophets:

> *Starting with Samuel, every prophet spoke about what is happening today.*   Acts 3:24

Samuel Knew the Voice of God:

Samuel's faith was, perhaps, revealed most clearly in the fact that because he knew the voice of God, he had no fear of men. He told Eli exactly what the Lord had shown him in the Temple, although the message involved the destruction of the household of the priest himself. He *"didn't hold anything back"*:

> *So Samuel told Eli everything; he didn't hold anything back (hid nothing from him, KJV).*   1 Samuel 3:18

Samuel was also not afraid to challenge King Saul:

> *When Samuel finally found him, Saul greeted him cheerfully. "May the LORD bless you," he said. "I have carried out the LORD's command!"*
> *"Then what is all the bleating of sheep and lowing of cattle I hear?" Samuel demanded.*
>   1 Samuel 15:13-14

195

When faced with the Philistines, Samuel prayed them into retreat:

Just as Samuel was sacrificing the burnt offering, the Philistines arrived for battle. But the LORD spoke with a mighty voice of thunder from heaven, and the Philistines were thrown into such confusion that the Israelites defeated them. The men of Israel chased them from Mizpah to Beth-car, slaughtering them all along the way. Samuel then took a large stone and placed it between the towns of Mizpah and Jeshanah. He named it Ebenezer — "the stone of help" — for he said, "Up to this point the LORD has helped us!" So the Philistines were subdued and didn't invade Israel again for a long time. And throughout Samuel's lifetime, the LORD's powerful hand was raised against the Philistines.

1 Samuel 7:10-13

What a great man of faith! Time and space does not permit us to tell more of his exploits. We are under the same restraints as the writer of Hebrews in his great P.S. to chapter 11.

WE HAVE MUCH TO LEARN

We have much to learn from all of these great men and women of faith, but we want to leave space to speak about your faith, for that is the important one at the moment. These men and women are all dead and gone to their reward. Their struggles have ended. It is you who are still here on earth, still breathing and still facing the challenges of everyday life.

But if Gideon, Barak, Samson, Jephthah, David and Samuel could all overcome in their day, then you, too, can face the seemingly impossible situations of your daily life and overcome. Say with me right now, and say it with faith, *"I Can Do This!"*

Now, go out and do it in Jesus' name.

PART III

BRINGING IT ALL HOME

CHAPTER 16

NOW, IT'S YOUR TURN

So, you see, it is impossible to please God without faith. Anyone who wants to come to him must believe that there is a God and that he rewards those who sincerely seek him.   Hebrews 11:6

It was a grand P.S., wasn't it? And what was the writer of Hebrews trying to tell us about Abel and Enoch and Noah and Abraham and Sarah and Isaac and Jacob and Joseph and Amram and Jochebed and Moses and Joshua and Rahab and Gideon and Barak and Samson and Jephthah and David and Samuel that we should remember? He said that they did the following:

- *Overthrew kingdoms*
- *Ruled with justice*

- *Received what God had promised them*
- *Shut the mouths of lions*
- *Quenched the flames of fire*
- *Escaped death by the edge of the sword*
- *[Had] their weakness ... turned to strength*
- *Became strong in battle*
- *Put whole armies to flight*
- *Received their loved ones back again from death*

(Hebrews 11:33-35)

And they did it all *"by faith."* None of these deeds was accomplished because of the mental capacity or natural talents of the individual involved, but through simple faith in God and through the obedience inspired by that simple faith.

SUFFERING IS A NORMAL PART OF THE CHRISTIAN LIFE

Another very important point is made here in Hebrews, one that many have chosen to ignore. The faith of these heroes was also shown in their willingness to suffer for what they believed to be right. Whether or not Christians should suffer anything has become a heated controversy among believers. Some are teaching that to suffer at all is a sign of a lack of faith, while others take a more traditional stance on this issue.

Since we live in the midst of a fallen race, the world has never understood those who love and trust God and has often treated them badly. The suffering this world has visited upon the people of God, however, was never interpreted as a sign that they lacked faith. Indeed, the phrase, *"Women received their dead raised to life again"* (KJV), is then followed by the phrase *"others were tortured, not accepting deliverance."* In the King James Version, these two statements are part of the very same sentence and the very same verse. While we need not invite the world's animosity, we can expect it, at times, and must accept it as a normal part of the Christian life.

Of these heroes, the writer says:

> *The faith of these heroes was also shown in their willingness to suffer for what they believed to be right!*

- *[They] were tortured, not accepting deliverance; that they might obtain a better resurrection.*
- *[They] had trial of cruel mockings and scourgings, yea, moreover of bonds and imprisonment.*
- *They were stoned.*
- *They were sawn asunder.*
- *[They] were tempted.*
- *[They] were slain with the sword.*
- *They wandered about in sheepskins and goatskins; being destitute, afflicted, tormented.*

- *They wandered in deserts, and in mountains, and in dens and caves of the earth.*
(Hebrews 11:35-38, KJV)

To some, these may not sound like the actions of victorious people of faith, yet Hebrews declares that *"the world was not worthy"* of such men and women (verse 38). Not once is the suffering of such saints mentioned in a derogatory way, as if they could have avoided it, if they'd only had enough faith. The opposite is true. They refused to avoid these sufferings—*because* they had faith.

DID JESUS HAVE ENOUGH FAITH?

If it were true that you could avoid all suffering if you just had enough faith, then maybe Jesus Himself didn't exercise enough faith. He suffered the wrath of this world and taught His disciples that they should also expect to suffer it:

Everyone will hate you because of your allegiance to me. But those who endure to the end will be saved.
Matthew 10:22

Then you will be arrested, persecuted, and killed. You will be hated all over the world because of your allegiance to me. Matthew 24:9

When the world hates you, remember it hated me before it hated you. The world would love you if you be-

*longed to it, but you don't. I chose you to come out of
the world, and so it hates you. Do you remember what
I told you? "A servant is not greater than the master."
Since they persecuted me, naturally they will perse-
cute you. And if they had listened to me, they would
listen to you! The people of the world will hate you
because you belong to me, for they don't know God
who sent me.*   John 15:18-21

Simple faith in God prepares us for every eventuality.
Therefore if trouble comes, we should take it in stride—
knowing that God has not changed, that His love for us
has not changed and that He is working in every circumstance for our benefit. As the Scriptures declare:

*And we know that God causes everything to work to-
gether for the good of those who love God and are called
according to his purpose for them.*   Romans 8:28

"*We know,*" and that should be enough.

Prospering in Good Times and in Bad

Faith causes us to be victorious—in good times and in
bad. It causes us to triumph—in times of lack and in
times of prosperity. The apostle Paul learned how to
prosper spiritually when things were going well and also
when they were not:

I have learned how to get along happily whether I have

much or little. I know how to live on almost nothing or with everything. I have learned the secret of living in every situation, whether it is with a full stomach or empty, with plenty or little. For I can do everything with the help of Christ who gives me the strength I need.

Philippians 4:11-13

> **When prosperity comes, simple faith keeps us humble and recognizing the Source of our blessings!**

Paul said, *"I have learned (am instructed, KJV)."* God had shown him both *"how to live on almost nothing (how to be abased, KJV)"* and also how to live *"with everything (how to abound, KJV),"* how to *"be full"* (KJV) and also how to *"be hungry"* (KJV), how to *"abound"* (KJV) and also how to *"suffer need"* (KJV). Wow!

HOW TO SUFFER AND HOW TO PROSPER

How to suffer and how to prosper are two extremes that most of us don't handle very well. We're fine, as long as life goes on more or less on an even keel, but when life chooses to throw us a curve, we find out quickly what we're really made of, and we're often not very pleased with what we see. Too often, we get discouraged and despondent and lose faith in God—when He's looking for just the opposite reaction. We all have much to learn in this regard.

In the same way that most of us have not learned to suffer, most of us also have not learned to prosper. Because prosperity brings with it new temptations, new demands for responsible behavior and new opportunities to flex one's muscles and make life-changing decisions, prosperity adversely affects many believers. Just as many fine Christian people are brought down by prosperity as are brought down by trouble, and maybe even more. It's not easy to suffer, and it's not easy to prosper, yet God wants to teach us how to handle both of these extremes.

When prosperity comes, simple faith can keep us humble and recognizing the Source of our blessings. It can make us confess that God is everything and that we are nothing. In this way, we can avoid the usual pitfalls of riches. Most of us, however, fall prey to the temptations of riches and, as a result, God must withhold His blessing from us for a time—because He loves us so much.

There is just as much teaching in the Bible about the dangers of riches as there are promises of prosperity. Doing well can be the greatest danger to the Christian life. Riches are far more dangerous to us than any demon we might be called to face.

Persecution Will Come

In the same way, one of the most prominent themes of the book of Acts (the only book of history in the New Testament) is the persecution and unwarranted suffering that the early Church experienced. More is said of persecution, for example, than of deliverance from demons, healing or even salvation. Suffering is part of the Christian life and comes to us because God loves us.

The apostle Paul declared:

For our present troubles (our light affliction, KJV) are quite small and won't last very long. Yet they produce for us an immeasurably great glory that will last forever! So we don't look at the troubles we can see right now; rather, we look forward to what we have not yet seen. For the troubles we see will soon be over, but the joys to come will last forever.

2 Corinthians 4:17-18

What we suffer now is nothing compared to the glory he will give us later.   Romans 8:18

People of faith can love God and stay happy when it rains and when it shines. They can be just as happy when their pockets are empty as when they're full. They can rejoice when people love them and cooperate with them, and they can still rejoice when people misunderstand them and work against them. Since simple faith is based upon an unchanging God, it cannot and must not be a wavering faith (based on the circumstances of the moment), or it is no faith at all.

Simple faith is the result of our intimacy with God, and nothing must be allowed to intrude upon the confidences we share with Him. Circumstances, bad or good, must never be permitted to affect how we relate to our Creator. He never changes, no matter what else changes around us, so our faith in Him must not change either.

Faith Is a Very Personal Thing

Faith is a very personal thing, and, in a very real sense, I cannot go further in telling you what your relationship with God should be. He requires something unique of each of us, so that the relationship of faith He enjoys with each person is different. He may not tell you to build an ark, to gather an army, to blow a trumpet, to march around the walls of Jericho, or any of the other things these men and women of the Bible did. He may not lead you to leave home and travel to a foreign country, to start churches in places that don't have them, to open a Bible school to train laborers for the harvest, or to write a book or establish a publishing ministry—as He has me. Your calling from God will be your calling and no one else's.

Therefore we cannot simply copy the faith of others or try to duplicate the things they're called to do. While we can learn from others, and I trust that you have learned and will continue to learn from the biblical heroes of faith, at some point you must stand on your own faith and choose to obey God on your own.

We can see from the experience of these men and women that it's important to get to know God and to hear His voice, that it's important to obey Him (even when every circumstance seems to be to the contrary) and that we don't need anything physical to prove to us what God can do. Our faith is all the *"evidence"* we need, and we require no further *"substance."*

But that's as far as I can go. Now, the rest is up to you. Will you find God trustworthy? Will you believe what He tells you? Will you prove your trust in Him by obeying His unique will for your life? Will you move forward, without requiring something more than your relationship of faith in the unfailing God? I trust that you will and that you will also, in time, be added to God's list of heroes.

If they, in their time, were able to overcome, then you, too, can face the seemingly impossible situations of your daily life and overcome. Say with me right now, and say it with faith, *"I Can Do This!"*

Now, go out and do it in Jesus' name.

For I can do everything with the help of Christ who gives me the strength I need.
Philippians 4:13

Anything is possible if a person believes.
Mark 9:23

MINISTRY PAGE

Readers may contact Harold and Andy McDougal in any of the following ways:

Mail:
Harold and Andrea "Andy" McDougal
1600 N Frost Street
Alexandria, VA 22304

Email: hmcdougal@verizon.net

www.thepublishedword.com

— Notes —

— NOTES —